A PENGUIN SPECIAL

THE ANIMALS REPORT

Richard North has been a journalist for the last ten years, after spending many years as a chauffeur, and van, lorry, security and ferry-boat driver. He also worked as a very contented part-time bicycle repairer in Kentish Town. He spent a year as a mature student at Cambridge, studying philosophy, but left to try to earn a living by writing. He is a frequent contributor to *The Times*, the *Radio Times* and the *Listener* among others, and he was, for its last year, the editor of *Vole*, the pioneer environmental paper. He is a co-author of *The Little Green Book: An Owner's Guide to the Planet* (1979) and author of the text to *Lord Lichfield's Unipart Calendar Book* (1982), and of a forthcoming book on the British wetlands.

Richard North nurtures an ambition to live on St David's Head in west Wales, but for the time being is happily ensconced in Hackney, east London. He is married with three young children.

THE ANIMALS REPORT

Richard North

Penguin Books

Penguin Books Ltd, Harmondsworth, Middlesex, England
Penguin Books, 40 West 23rd Street, New York, New York 10010, U.S.A.
Penguin Books Australia Ltd, Ringwood, Victoria, Australia
Penguin Books Canada Ltd, 2801 John Street, Markham, Ontario, Canada L3R 1B4
Penguin Books (N.Z.) Ltd, 182–190 Wairau Road, Auckland 10, New Zealand

First published 1983

Printed and bound in Great Britain by
Cox & Wyman Ltd, Reading

Set in VIP Palatino by
Northumberland Press Ltd, Gateshead

CONTENTS

PREFACE

There never was a better time to rethink our attitudes towards animals. Activists of every kind, and of every degree of eccentricity, are claiming our attention for abuses to animals of every sort. Some of them do it by breaking the law just a little bit (say, in raiding laboratories). Some – none of whom are officially recognized by any known group that a journalist can contact – mail letter-bombs (apparently, some of them at least are obvious fakes) to well-known people. On a more intellectual level, others – notably the 1983 BBC *Horizon* lecturer, Professor Peter Singer – exhort us to take our philosophical duty towards animals more seriously.

Prompted by well-orchestrated, persistent (and often extraordinarily boring) heckling at their public meetings, and by constant, cleverly organized political pressure, politicians have gradually come to accept that it is wise to appear to be in sympathy with animal welfare issues. Animal welfare, like the environment, is something which it is best to be in favour of. And, like the environment, it is something which has proved to be very easy to ignore or to abuse when the burdens of office are on ministers.

However, animal welfare issues – and environmental issues – will not now go away. The ardent campaigners are only the most vociferous among the millions of people in this country who have come to see that their relations with the rest of Creation – its animals and landscapes and biological well-being – are of profound consequence. They are issues of practical and spiritual concern which fly rather too directly in the face of many of the material demands to which we have fallen prey.

For myself, I would like to stress that animals are, like us, an integral part of the wider biosphere for which we have a unique responsibility (since, unlike animals, we have a potential for taking responsibility). It is important to mention, though, that animals have a unique claim on us because of their ability to feel pain.

I have been tempted into the discussion because I found that I was worried about my own ignorance of animals. For instance, I was surprised to find that I, like most 'townies', had not realized that a cow's calves are taken from her so that we, and not they, can drink the milk from her teats (some go to their deaths immediately so that we can steal their mothers' milk without the burden of feeding the creatures it was intended for). Such ignorance results in our causing animals suffering for our own convenience with hardly a qualm.

I wanted to address myself to that ignorance, and diminish it. But I must also say that it was not solely a mission of do-gooding which brought me to the subject. I was brought to it because it is most extraordinarily interesting. Animals are, of course, interesting in themselves, but our relations with them are clearly mostly out of kilter, and are also in themselves extremely interesting.

Beyond these factors, and beyond even the fact that animals matter because they can suffer, I was fascinated by the entire business of the way this society – my own, much-loved tribe – is coming to grips with its burgeoning unease on the subject. I hope nobody would ever be able to accuse me of taking a *sociological* interest in a subject (sociology being the appalling trade of treating people as though they were social machines); but it was certainly something like amateur anthropology which brought me to these themes.

This is a journalistic book. It was written by someone who is concerned, but not an expert, who professes only the small skill of getting hold of good informants and wringing information out of them. At the same time, however, the views in it are my own: they are the views of someone who listened to experts and then formed a sort of saloon-bar overview. More than that, I should say that the mistakes in the book are very much my own.

Naturally, I owe a very great deal to the patience of the people from whom I begged sometimes long hours of conversation. Especially, I owe a debt to Christopher Turton and Jim Morrish, farmers both, who allowed me to visit their farms, even though they knew me to be critical of animal farming. Their openness, kindness and generosity made the 'Animal Farm' chapter possible.

Richard Ryder, David MacDonald, Angela Walder, Alan Long, Bill Jordan, Clive Hollands, Marian Dawkins, Sheila Silcock, Jonathan Barzdo, Stefan Ormrod and Colin Booty were all kind enough to read different bits of the book and offer their advice and help, even when they disagreed with some or all of what they saw. Some of their advice was taken. And some, perhaps too much, was ignored. All the kinder of them to put up with being treated in so cavalier a fashion.

To Philips I owe the invaluable aid of a word-processor, without which the manuscript would have been even later and scrappier, and – if possible – even more of a burden to Michael Dover of Penguin, who has done much to give the project shape.

To Anne, my wife, I owe the peace and quiet with which to work: a miraculous woman, indeed, who can bring forth such splendid children and then keep them in so cheerful a frame of mind that they never seem to constitute a really good excuse for their father to be unable to get on with his work.

Hackney, November 1982

INTRODUCTION

At different times and in different cultures, the human race has held very different attitudes towards animals. They have been held to be miraculous symbols of the gentleness of the natural creation and, almost in the same breath, of its savagery. They have been held as beings untainted by guilt and free from Original Sin, and they have been drawn as demon spirits. They have been our greatest friends and our most feared enemies. They have been regarded as good, loyal and quaint, and at the same time symbolic of the dark, apocalyptic, barbarian innerness of human beings and Creation.

Different animals are given their own characteristics: there are wily serpents and gambolling lambs; satanic goats and adoring labradors; roaring lions and workman-like horses. Some animals combine opposing characters: the cat purring on the spinster's hearth; the witch's cat companion.

Hardly surprising, then, that double-think abounds. It is a measure of the peculiar position that animals hold in our minds that we use them in our most familiar religious images (the Good Shepherd and His flock), but we breed and rear them in desperately crowded thousands for our dining-tables or laboratories. We teach our children through the literature of nursery books that animals live pleasantly in spacious farmyards and fields, while we feed them animal food produced callously in factories. We affect to love animals, but we abuse them routinely. Now, however, there is an emerging awareness that animals have never suffered so commonly and that we have never stood in greater need of a decent relationship with the animal kingdom around us.

This book charts the major abuses to which we subject animals, and tries to show the situations in which we abuse animals for very trivial reasons, and where, on the other hand, their suffering seems capable of moral defence. Not many people will agree with all the conclusions, and on the whole I have preferred to chart the dilemmas and provide the information rather than persuade the reader as to what he or she should think. It is in some sense, though, a piece of propaganda. I do believe that much of the misery which we impose on animals could be stopped overnight were it not for our greed and laziness.

The first chapter, 'What are Animals Like?', discusses what we know about animals. The evidence is more speculative than we might like, but it leaves one in little doubt that animals clearly matter. They *can* suffer. Once one knows that, one knows that they matter in themselves, quite apart from any value they may have for us. That we know they matter because they suffer is not a strictly philosophically sound proposition, but I think it will suffice for all ordinary purposes.

Chapter 2, 'Animal Farm', is a guide to what happens in the production of animal foods. Very few of us need to eat any animal produce at all. Almost all of us in the West eat far too much. This is the area of animal abuse in which, if one could do such a sum, one would say that by far the greatest suffering, for by far the least human purpose, takes place. If you read this chapter and remain a contented meat-eater and milk-drinker, then I have failed. Perhaps I should have drawn the scenes more graphically.

'Animals in Laboratories' was potentially an even grimmer chapter than 'Animal Farm'. It is tough enough, in all conscience. The issues are complex and the dilemmas very sharp. This chapter will have served well enough if it charts the areas in which laboratory animals are used profligately and foolishly. And even more, it will have been useful if readers are persuaded to lobby (or support those who lobby) for a very great deal more public accountability for animal researchers.

'Zoos, Circuses and Wildness' charts the peculiar abuse to which we subject animals which satisfy our curiosity about the exotic – mostly foreign – wild creatures. This is a bizarre cruelty, since we normally profess to enjoy seeing 'wild' animals because they are so magnificent and different from us. But thousands of people seem to be content to watch them being humiliated in environments in which no shred of naturalness or magnificence is allowed them, or in which they cavort grotesquely to human command.

And so to 'Pets, Pests and the Pursued'. This chapter aims to unravel some of the double standards with which we regard the animals with which we share our environment. These are not the creatures we imprison in cages, whether in factory farms, laboratories, zoos or circuses. These are the wildlife creatures we pursue or photograph; the pets with whom we share our gardens; the rats in our sewers; the mink and cats who escape and live feral lives. They must bear the brunt of some peculiar attitudes: animals killed by kindness, or made miserable by our impetuous curiosity. They show us how extraordinarily dependent on humans, on the one hand, and independent of them, on the other, different animals can be. Some animals vary their relationship to humans at their own convenience; others have all too little choice over how their lives intertwine with ours.

Yet humans, at least some of them, do try to help animals. Chapter 6, 'Campaigners', looks at the men and women who set their hearts on helping animals. They are an eccentric lot, much given to furious rows among themselves, but many of them are extraordinarily brave.

The Conclusion speaks for itself.

WHAT ARE ANIMALS LIKE?

Sentiency and intelligence have always been the criteria which people have used to try to consider what other animals are like, and whether they have any claim on us. We know much more now than, for instance, the Ancient Greeks, but we are similarly divided on the upshot. Oddly, it is not so much the feelings of animals that are in dispute, as what to do about the evidence that they do feel. The human race is rational enough to seek for evidence of this or that; it is seldom rational enough to act upon it. In the end, animals need sentimentalists if they are to be defended from the ravages of human exploitation.

It seems, very roughly, that there is no animal so stupid that it does not deserve our consideration. It seems also that there are few people so considerate that they do not daily and trivially abuse the animal kingdom's deserts. Nonetheless, animals are very different from people, and it is important to see that whatever else makes animals a charge upon us, it is not their sameness with us that creates our responsibilities to them.

Descartes said that there are few people so stupid that they cannot speak, and no animal so wise that it could speak. Animals were machines, and not even machines with a spark of divinity, like human beings. But Descartes was an honest man and admitted:

> But though I regard it as established that we cannot prove there is any thought in animals, I do not think it is thereby proved that there is not, since the human mind does not reach into their hearts.

This would not do for an equally thinking person, equally driven by their formidable intellect. Here is Voltaire:

Barbarians seize this dog, which in friendship surpasses man so prodigiously; they nail it on a table, and they dissect it alive in order to show the mesenteric veins. You discover in it all the same organs of feeling that are in yourself. Answer me, machinist, has nature arranged all the means of feeling in this animal, so that it may not feel? . . . Do not suppose this impertinent contradiction in nature.

And indeed David Hume, keen to have the human being as a creature whose intellect comes already imprinted (as we might say, or 'programmed'), sees no difficulty at all in comparing its intellect with that of an animal, or vice versa.

But the great arguments about people and animals were bedevilled by other problems: are animals, like people, divine, or is the very opposite true? The Catholic Church was usually keen to say that animals were certainly not divine, but ought to be treated well as a mark of our own decency and respect for Creation (but not always: in the nineteenth century, at least one lesser theologian, the Jesuit Fr Joseph Rickaby, and a pope, Pius IX, thought that animals could be abused with impunity, though the latter believed that acts of wanton cruelty were bad things in themselves).

Leaving aside the worrying over whatever share of divinity it is that animals share with people (and the modern Church, which has declared St Francis the patron of ecology, has come a long way in this respect), we are more likely to enjoy Schopenhauer's view that, in trying to inflate the role of reason in human beings, earlier philosophers found it all too convenient to understate that of animals. But, as Schopenhauer said pointedly:

If any Cartesian were to find himself clawed by a tiger, he would become aware in the clearest possible manner of the sharp distinction such a beast draws between its ego and the non-ego.

He goes on to notice that such philosophers often found themselves using special words for the things which animals do, but which people also do, in order to drive a distinction between the non-human societies and us. Perhaps there is a similarity here between modern scientists and the earlier philosophers: it is easier to forget the power of screams of agony and distress when they are described as 'vocalization', the mealy-mouthed word which modern animal experimenters use for any animal utterance.

People and animals are closer to one another than many of us like to imagine. Konrad Lorenz's *On Aggression* is not the brilliant piece of philosophizing that some people took it for when it came out in 1966; but it is an extraordinary essay about the similarity of the ways in which animals and people bind together to face a common enemy or form bonds of trust between individuals, perhaps more safely to produce families, perhaps to fend off loneliness and perhaps to express an inner desire not to be lonely (and perhaps simply as an attempt to undo the solipsism which certainly afflicts the talking animals). But Lorenz's description of the social life of greylag geese, on which he is the acknowledged world expert, opens up immense speculation. For instance, here is Lorenz on the occasional goose which failed to find a proper lover on whom to pour out that bird's considerable capacity for constancy and devotion:

Permanently unrequited, unhappy love is the fate of those who become attached to individuals whose affections are already absorbed in a happy mating. Ganders, in this case, very soon desist from their unsuccessful courtship; at least I have never known one to pursue a well-mated female for years. The record of a very tame hand-reared female, on the other hand, shows that her faithful love for a happily mated gander persisted for more than four years.

There is something here to suggest that humans should not allow their interest in animals to bring them to interfere in the animals' lives: this is, after all, a hand-reared bird we are talking about. Perhaps she had been left only with enough 'gooseness' in her nature to fall in love with the gander, but had been robbed of the goose common-sense to find an appropriate mate. This is also a problem with chimpanzees who are handled too much, perhaps in zoos, for advertising gimmicks, with photographers or in 'language-learning' experiments.

It appears from Lorenz's work that geese do make faithful lovers (vindicating to some extent the Paul Gallico story, *Snow*

Goose, which has brought successive generations to tears). We may not want to talk about 'love' as applied to geese, especially as 'promiscuity' or faithfulness in animals can be explained in terms of natural selection. But if a goose's partner dies and the bereft one goes around moping, we call it mourning, just as much as we call the anger which humans and animals share at certain moments aggression. Why should a goose be allowed the description 'aggressive' when it attacks a threatening creature, but not 'loving' when it maintains a tenacious and supportive long-term relationship and mourns its mate when death or disaster parts them?

In very many cases animals appear to be quite like us, or we like them (depending on whether knowing about the similarity inclines you to 'upgrade' animals or 'downgrade' humans in order to bring them to a proper proximity). Of course, none of this is to undo the fact that it is I, and not a goose, that can sit down and write a book on the similarities and differences between my species and all the others.

The gorilla has a brain of about half the weight of a human's. A monkey's brain has several billion nerve cells; a human's has ten billion or more. Some threadworms, fairly lowly creatures, have less than a few hundred nerve cells. But brain size is not a reliable guide to what is going on inside them: Turgenev's brain weighed over 2,000 grams, while Anatole France's weighed half that. Who is to say that it made much difference?

There are different sorts of brain, of course. Normally, an animal's brain seems to be related to its size (thus elephants have very much bigger brains than ours). But a human's brain is three times the size that would have been expected by this (very rough) rule, taking into account his body weight. And it seems that in human beings a smaller proportion of the brain is 'dedicated' (to use a computing term) to simple body-control functions. In other words, it has spare capacity, over and above normal mammalian requirements, for ratiocination, language and so on. Moreover, it seems – though the issue is shrouded in controversy – that just as an animal often knows how to hunt without ever having seen any animal do any hunting, humans have a capacity for language which is not explained by anything like picking it up. Language seems to flow from us like musical composition from a prodigy.

The nervous system and the brain are inextricably linked: the brain is highly concentrated and consists of organized groups of the kind of cells which make up nervous systems. There are creatures which respond to stimuli (advancing towards food, retreating from danger) which we do not imagine to have brains – the hydra, for instance. We do not know whether they feel and, if so, what they feel. We know only that they respond. Since this is also in a sense true of what we know of our fellow humans, it does not give us confidence that we can judge that simple creatures do not feel, or that what they feel does not constitute exactly the kind of pain known to us.

The humblest hydra, a minuscule water metazoan, has a nerve net. 'The reactions possible in such a system are quite restricted, but the nerve net is at least a step in the evolution towards mentality,' says biologist Garrett Hardin. Such a creature does not have anything that could be quite called a brain; but move on up to the world of worms and molluscs and we immediately encounter the planaris: only a few millimetres in length, they do, however, have a brain. Planaria can learn: they will avoid turning in whichever direction at the top of a T-tube lies a sharp tap with a stick. At the evolutionary level of the bee we have creatures which can make complicated navigational manoeuvres and communicate with fellow bees about the direction and distance to, and quality of, a source of nectar. However, we know nothing about what any of this range of experience 'feels' like to an animal.

The evidence about animals' brain power is, at least some of it, peculiar. It depends equally on what we know, and on what we do not know. We know that 'lower' animals have nervous systems. They are nothing like as quick in operation as ours, or as those of other higher animals, nor are they as complex, and they do not connect with much of a brain. We know that the creatures react to stimuli and seem to have a capacity to learn. We know that quite humble animals (like the bee) have remarkable powers. All of this leads to there being plausibility behind the notion that every creature from a flatworm 'up' may well have the capacity for pain. They may not get much warning of it by sensory awareness; they may not think much or anything at all about it; and they certainly can't tell us anything about it (except perhaps by their flinching); but they may well be experiencing pain for all that. We do not have the means to think about such things: our experience of pain is so much complicated by the capacity to say to ourselves or someone else, 'I am in pain'; to resent it and wish it would go away; to feel it undeserved; or to pray for relief. We have pain, and we have self-consciousness about pain. We assume such cognitive skills to be a function of the 'spare' capacity that we know we have in our brains. But that we have a different sort of consciousness does not let us off the problem that the pain itself is also there, and so may it be in quite lowly creatures.

Modern science has less to say about pain than one might expect. Professors Ronald Melzack and Patrick Wall are perhaps the leading experts on the subject, and have just worked together to update the classic work on the subject, *The Puzzle of Pain*, written by Ronald Melzack in 1973 (the new book is called *The Challenge of Pain*). Much of what they say is not easily accessible to the layman, but it becomes clear even to a scientific ignoramus that, in the higher mammals at least, the mechanism of pain is complex and not at all to be explained by the simple Cartesian approach, whose metaphor is a man on the end of a rope (the stimulus) pulling hard enough to ring the church bells (the painful sensation), in which the nerve ending is the bell-ringer, the spinal cord the rope, and the brain the church bells.

The brain is able to produce endomorphins and encephalins which appear to mitigate pain. The brain seems able to tranquillize the experience that it feels, in a kind of dialogue between the brain and pain in which the brain is able – at least temporarily – to mitigate the full rigours of what it experiences, even before they have begun (people in car accidents often do not feel pain, so swift is the brain's ability to dull it for a while.)

A picture emerges of very peculiar and, for the time being, indecipherable processes and interactions. We know rather little about pain in people, and even less about pain in animals. However, we do know that the pain physiology of humans is shared by all but the very simplest of animal organisms.

It is important here to note that anyone who does not believe that pain in animals matters, as though theirs is fundamentally different in type and quality from human pain, ought at the very least to consider carefully, in that case, how it is that animals are used as human substitutes and models in pain research. Either they are like us and relevant, and therefore matter; or they are very different and irrelevant, and may perhaps not matter.

In an experiment initiated in 1980 some laboratory rats were injected with substances which gave them the painful condition of rheumatoid arthritis, the symptoms of which they displayed along with the distress which would be expected with such an experience. All the differences in behaviour of these rats – all the ways in which their new (probably pained) behaviour differed from that of others which had not been given the condition – were monitored. They were then given pain-relievers of the sort that work with human beings, and their behaviour began to return to 'normal'. By such means do scientists come to the kind of proof without which they would be uncomfortable in taking the pain of animals seriously. Scientists have been trained to measure things and are unfortunately all too able to ignore phenomena (especially when they are phenomena happening to an animal) if they cannot be, or have not been, measured.

This is the behavioural approach: it considers ways of assessing the miseries which an animal endures by observing the behaviour of animals in certain situations. It is a science which has grown very much recently, led by the relatively new discipline of ethology (the study of animal behaviour) under the inspiration of Konrad Lorenz at Vienna and Niko Tinbergen at Cambridge as the elder statesmen of the trade. In 1965 a British ethologist, W. H. Thorpe, wrote a paper entitled 'Assessment of Pain and Distress in Animals', which has since been much quoted as providing a basis for thinking about the sufferings which animals may endure.

There are two opposite pitfalls which beset those who, like ourselves, attempt to decide upon the limits of physical injury and restraint which it is not permissible for a civilized people to exceed in their treatment of domestic animals. The first is the error of supposing that domestic animals in their feelings and anxieties are essentially like human beings; the second is the equally serious error of assuming that they are mere insentient automata.

Thorpe went on to say that humans have a particularly developed capacity to dread the future, but that some animals have some capacity in that direction; and that many of our domestic animals live highly developed social lives in their wild state, which we presumably disrupt at some peril to their happiness. He found himself wondering whether stress was always bad: human beings respond to and enjoy some forms of stress, and perhaps animals too might prefer some stress to a life of suffocating tedium. But who can tell? He was driven back to considering the origin of various species and wondering how different was their current domesticated life to that of their ancestors. It is not a fool-proof basis for conjecture about an animal's well-being, but it has one great merit: whatever an animal's life was like until we human beings came along (whether it was happy or not), it was at least not our fault. Thus, if we recreate their ancestral life as nearly as possible while we utilize them, we may or may not be making them happy; but it seems probable that we are at least making them, by our specific agency, no more or less happy than 'nature', Creation or God had made them before our intervention.

These sorts of comparison are not helpful to the intensive farmer. He habitually provides an environment which is not remotely like the animal's wild-state experience; that much is obvious. And Thorpe found that there was precious little evidence for the view that the domesticated animals were fundamentally different to their ancestors. As for sheep:

We can say that probably the sheep is the least affected by domestication of any of the ungulates.

On cattle, he commented:

As with other domestic animals, selective breeding has produced many changes in temperament and excitability, but there seems to be no evidence for a substantial change in any single innate behaviour pattern or instinctive need.

And on pigs:

The domestic pig seems to have been changed only in minor ways by the long process of domestication. The general temperament, whether 'lively' or 'dull', is certainly to a considerable extent under the control of the breeder, as are some parts of the sexual behaviour. Otherwise the domestic pig seems to show almost all the needs, drives, abilities and intelligence of its wild ancestor.

The lesson seems to be that, whatever else is going on, the creatures who share our lives with us are remarkably like the creatures we brought into the primitive pens of the first herdsman seven or eight thousand years ago. Whatever they wanted then, it seems they are likely still to want now. But we know little about it, and even less whether we satisfy them in ways which nature had not provided for thousands of years ago but which we find convenient to give them now; things such as a consistently dry environment, for example.

Professor Thorpe ended his discussion with a quotation from Lord Brain:

I personally can see no reason for conceding mind to my fellow men and denying it to animals ... Mental functions, rightly viewed, are but servants of the impulses and emotions by which we live, and these, the springs of life, are surely diencephalic in their neurological location. Since the diencephalon is well developed in animals and birds, I, at least, cannot doubt that the interests and activities of animals are correlated with awareness and feelings in the same way as my own, and which may be, for ought I know, just as vivid.

But how do we know, and what questions can we reasonably ask?

Ethologists and animal behaviourists are doing their best to construct experiments in which they can 'ask' animals what they (the animals) want. At Oxford University's Animal Behaviour Research Group, Marian Dawkins has been engaged in this kind of work for several years, and her *Animal Suffering* is the best pulling-together of contemporary understanding on the subject. Her own most well-known work is in giving chickens choices between battery-style captivity and something approaching free-range life. They prefer free-range life, but there are difficulties. For instance, as Konrad Lorenz discussed, animals like the familiar. The hen which knew only battery cages took a while to discover the joys of the free-range run, while the hen who had always known free-range life was never in any doubt. But the matter could be complicated considerably, Marian Dawkins found, by an attempt to find out what a hen would do if there was the advantage of food to be had from one or other of the cage sizes and types. She found that they went without food for a while if to eat meant going against their preference for location. But if they were a bit hungry, they went where the food was.

This sounds like crazy research. Who of us doubts that hens would rather live in ways which satisfy the immemorial promptings of their red jungle fowl ancestors from Borneo, which enjoy flying, rooting about and periods of harem-life followed by solitary periods when broody?

Firstly, of course, the poultry industry would like us to believe that hens have become habitués of their cages and prefer them. A poultry man argued in BBC TV's *Down on the Factory Farm* that hens had changed genetically in this direction, in spite of evidence that, given freedom (wanted or not), even battery hens will revert to fully fledged scratching, preening, hierarchical creatures after a period of adjustment. Work that goes towards establishing what hens want has the merit that it hinders the public-relations people who would like to be free to state as fact what is merely conjecture or convenient prejudice.

But there is another and deeper difficulty. It is that what we want for animals, if based on anthropomorphic intuition, can be very wrong-headed. In the mid sixties the Brambell Committee on the welfare of farm animals had been worried that the narrow-gauge wire of battery cages was uncomfortable to hens' feet. They recommended that a wider gauge be used, even though it had apparently been shown that more eggs would be lost in such a system. Researchers subsequently gave hens the choice of two sorts of floor and found that they stood for longer without shifting their feet on the narrow-gauge wire; and they showed also that, contrary to expectation, the narrow-gauge wire actually provided better support.

We have a fine balance here. Clearly, many scientists will devise and conduct experiments to prove the most banal and self-evident fact, and to measure it with a precision which is either useless or meaningless. But at the same time, if that is the only way to get simple truths accepted by the scientific community, then perhaps we have to accept that price. More importantly, we know so little about animals that the very least we can do is to make every effort to understand them as best we can. It is of course true that the way to avoid all sorts of animal miseries is to cease to exploit animals; but while society does exploit them, it behoves those that worry about their sufferings to come up with the evidence that animals suffer, and suffer in ways which can be avoided.

There is a good deal of work going on now to try to understand better what animals are doing in the wild: the intricacies of the family lives of a range of animals from foxes to cats are becoming clearer after the painstaking work of a new generation of researchers, many of whom – like David MacDonald at Oxford – are using radio tracking to 'stay with' animals whose secret lives no one can see. Many of these people agree that their work has some toll in animal inconvenience or worse, and worry about making their findings with as little intrusion as possible. After all, the little we know about animals is that whether they are like us or not, and in whatever ways and with whatever differences, our influence in their lives has far more often been destructive than otherwise.

We can be as certain that animals feel pain as that our human neighbours do. That fact alone ought to make us respect them. For the rest, our ignorance about animals ought to make us more, rather than less, respectful of their feelings.

2

ANIMAL FARM

My idea of the perfect lunch was born in a farmhouse in the village of Lubersac in Lot-et-Garonne. It is compounded of many things: getting up at dawn to go into the fields to work, before the sun has warmed away the dew; working on until the sun is high, the muscles tired and the mind bored. Lunch begins to loom as a prospect. It is to be a special lunch: relatives are coming in from town to celebrate the approaching completion of a successful harvest. All week we have eaten chickens and rabbits and guinea fowl and pork and eggs from the acre or so near the house. In the barn where four young men of the Maquis were shot in the Second World War, there is a goat whose milk produces a perfect chocolate rice-pudding which I am always given, having expressed a preference for it.

But on this special day we are to have a piece of meat which has not come from the farm. These people are peasants, and for them the celebratory meal demands something which they have not grown (whereas in England, of course, the exact reverse would be the case).

The first three or four courses of lunch proceed as usual. Vegetable soup to assuage the first, vulgar pangs of hunger, then bread, salads, pâté, and a special potato dish which has a garnish of egg and vinaigrette. But we are already discussing how to cook the perfectly bound, round, pink piece of butcher's beef. Amid much anxiety, advice and even abuse from anyone opposing her current whim, Madame, who is consulting everyone, wins through. Her idea is that the meat be lightly fried in a closed pan in half an inch of butter for a few minutes. It is suddenly transferred to a very hot oven for about fifteen minutes. And then it is served: pale, blushing and so tender that one has only to trail the blade across the meat and it is cut.

I have become a vegetarian of sorts since this encounter, and the hardest job is to resist the occasional treat of this kind. I know that I would like to be let off the hook, and be told that there is no suffering involved in the animal-products business, and believe it.

Apart from my annual month in the French countryside, I have also had the good fortune to work as a part-time shepherd in the Welsh hills. There we were used to pulling lambs that were too fat from their mothers. We did it carefully enough, I suppose, and we had the drugs with which to clean biologically the uteruses that we had sometimes rather roughly plundered. The alternative would often have been the death of the lambs and sometimes the mothers. They were happy days, spent amongst friends in beautiful surroundings and coming to grips with what seemed a very traditional and splendid way of life. The ritual of shepherding was very satisfying. We were proud that we lost fewer lambs than most of our neighbours. The farmer I worked with knew more than they did, and his wife was renowned for miles around for the tenderness and diligence with which she could manage difficult deliveries.

But after a while one comes to see that the lambs were systematically too big for their mothers: they were too well fed and developed by the time of their birth. And sometimes we not merely had to round the sheep up to move them from one field to the next – we quite often had to chase a suspected difficult case. It can be an arduous affair, for even a sheep with a lamb's nose peeping out at its rear can be very fleet and determined. Eventually we would bring the thing down, often with the deft use of a crook.

Sheep do not give much indication that they are in pain. The most you hear is a muted moan as the lamb is pulled out. The noise is a deep, subterranean cry, and it stops the moment the lamb is on the ground. We lost some lambs to the weather and some to the crows. Once, we lost some to the badgers. Even the local expert, who knew badgers and their ways, and delighted in watching them, agreed that the sett must be blocked off and gas applied. He was no happy huntsman, but he did the job.) Had we been aware, it would have worried us that the average British farm loses one in five of its lambs within three months of their birth, and a million a year are estimated to die within a couple of days of birth from cold, starvation or exposure.

If the sheep had bad feet, we clipped them till the blood flowed. If they had messy, dried dung on the wool at their rears (the expression for such rear-ends was 'caggly'), we would clip it off till the udder and anus at least were fairly decently clear. Sometimes, but not often, we clipped too close and had to spray the nick with antiseptic. At shearing time, the sheep had to endure rough herding and the peculiarity of being hoisted on to their backs so that the shearer could rid them of their fleece. The male lambs were usually castrated by a rubber-band device and had their tails docked; this was done while they were very young and at a cost in pain which cannot easily be judged.

For the rest of their time, they had lives which fulfilled everyone's picture-card idea of the countryside. The lambs really did gambol and frolic, playing the games for which sheep are famous and through which it appears they learn how to operate as a flock. The clear spring sun shone on their early days (though sometimes it was mixed with icy rain, several degrees of frost and a high wind). The lambs which went for slaughter lived on lush green grass, and the rest of the flock went up to their traditional mountain ranges for the summer.

I do not know what the sheep felt as we did the various jobs which a shepherd must perform to keep his flock hale. Probably far more of our sheep survived their early months than would have been the case in the 'wild'. But, on the other hand, whatever privations we forced upon those sheep, it is clear that *we* made them endure them. They were our fault. Just as in the business of animal experimentation, it is no good at all taking some imaginary sum of miseries which an animal must take as part of its 'wild' or 'natural' state and say that we can make it undergo a similar quantum of misery before any blame attaches to us. Firstly, the sum cannot be done: we do not know how to do it. Secondly, almost all the practices we perform are done so as massively to increase the numbers of a given species, so we are forever inflicting a degree of misery on more and more creatures. Thirdly, we are usually selecting for meat production rather than hardiness: our farm animals are being bred to be less and less good at surviving inclement weather or even their own unaided birth-giving.

The French peasant farmer, eating animals that he has carefully tended in a farming which is far from intensive, may have some justification in his animal-eating, and I certainly would not know how to resist sampling my Lubersac friends' daily fare. It is very seldom that they buy in the kind of beef which I so enjoyed and which doubtless involved much cruelty. But hardly any animal farming in Britain is conducted in their relatively benign way. Increasingly it is intensive farming which dominates.

The intensive methods are likely to be applied to larger numbers of a larger variety of species. In recent years, hardly any animal has escaped intensive production: they range from Albanian snails through to American alligators. The Institute of Aquaculture at Stirling University has been helping prisoners at Saughton Prison, Edinburgh, in their project to breed tilapia (reputed to be the fish which Jesus used to feed the five thousand). Many fish species are now commonly farmed intensively, in spite of the propensity of many of them – trout, for instance – to be far-ranging creatures which are given to sudden bouts of mass hysteria and deaths in captivity. There are reports of captive breeding of baby lobsters which are 'brought on' in the sea, and hatcheries of scallops have been developed. One Scottish landowner has a million farmed oysters in a corner of Loch Fyne.

There is a developing trend to farm deer, though – thanks largely to the intervention of the British Veterinary Association, and the Farm Animal Welfare Council (a government quango) – their velvet cannot now be sold to Orientals seeking its supposed aphrodisiac effects. Currently, seventy farms produce almost as much venison as is shot wild, perhaps 2,000 tons. Researchers are said to be hopeful that this figure will rise until venison makes up perhaps 5 per cent of Scotland's meat

production, utilizing wilderness land but very probably with
increasing temptations to intensification.

No one could have predicted the intensification of British
sheep farming. But now a growing number of sheep-farmers
follow common Scandinavian practice and bring their sheep in
to sheds for the latter part of the winter, shear them and look
forward to easier lambing in the spring. A sheep without its
wool requires 20 per cent less space. Rabbits (British farmers sell
half their production abroad) and goats are both receiving more
commercial attention too.

According to a 1981 British Association conference paper by
Professor G. E. Lamming, 'Animal production in the twenty-
first century' (not published), animals produce around two
thirds of the agricultural production of this country (cattle and
milk contribute nearly 40 per cent of total agricultural output,
sheep and wool 4 per cent; pigs 9 per cent; and poultry and eggs
12 per cent). Noting a dramatic increase in yields, the professor
says 'there is no reason why these increases cannot continue',
and he predicts an increase in intensification. We may yet try to
produce beef on the American feedlot system, though some of
the beef-producing enterprises on a huge scale have actually
caught a cold there. The National Farmers' Union may yet be
able to announce dramatic 'improvements' on the Poultry
Worker of the Year Award given to a farmer in 1980 for manag-
ing to squeeze an average 335 eggs from each of his flock in a
63-week period. And doubtless we shall find ways to increase
hormonological ingenuity (between £10 million and £20
million per year is already being spent on chemically increasing
flesh production).

The British Association paper eulogizes medication techniques which will serve the same purpose as castration, the fate
of the majority of male animals which makes them rather more
manageable and produces meat which is paler (but no tastier
and with no proven market advantage). Techniques coming
along now may also produce a hormonological contraceptive
effect, and even tamper with the mechanism of growth control,
so that giant-sized animals can be produced. Already farmers
like to promote fast growth so that the animal is ready for sale

30

before any of the meat 'taints' (usually darkening and streaki-
ness) associated with post-puberty appear. They are able to cite
the avoidance of the 'need' for castration as a welfare benefit
from these developments. Though the public appear to be
indifferent to the taints in, say, boar meat, the butchers still
insist that the pigs they buy be free from them.

It is now virtually impossible to be sure that the animal
product which one eats has been produced with any serious
consideration being given to humane methods of production,
rather than cheapness for the consumer and profit for the producer. Only in the case of eggs has there been any attempt
specially to label merchandise which has been so produced.
Martin Pitt, the biggest producer of free-range eggs in the
country, labels each of his 9,500 daily eggs: 'Free range – Martin
Pitt'.) The first and crucial reform that should come from the
public's increased awareness that animals suffer on farms is a
trustworthy system whereby they can know that they are buying decently produced meat, milk and eggs. It would not matter
if such food was more expensive: we are mostly eating more
than is good for us and could easily and healthily eat less for our
food expenditure.

The rest of this chapter looks at the facts of animal farming,
and some of the myths perpetrated about it. Most of the
sections deal with an aspect of intensification, with special
reference to a particular type of farm animal (the 'Intensification' section especially deals with hens; 'Intensive production,
money and pollution' with pigs; and 'The farm animal myth'
with cows).

Feeding the masses

During one year the average Briton now consumes more than
his or her own weight in meat, according to Dr Alan Long, the
honorary scientific officer of the Vegetarian Society. That adds
up to 8 beef animals, 36 pigs, 36 sheep and 550 poultry birds in
the average lifetime. Roughly 35 million eggs a day are consumed in Britain. Our animal population on farms is around 55
million (excluding chickens, which number around 130 million)

31

and 3,000 animals a minute are killed throughout every working day.

The increasing affluence of the vast majority of British citizens has lifted them from the malnutrition of, say, the 1880s to a new kind of malnutrition in which, though they eat more and more of many good things like vegetables and fruit (per capita consumption of which has doubled in the last century, though it is still low by Continental or American standards), they eat, roughly speaking, half the wheat flour, five times the poultry and game, a third more milk, well over twice the amount of meat and three times as many eggs as their great-grandparents. At least, in spite of assiduous promotions, the consumption of milk and butter is now declining. But cheese, on the other hand, maintains its share of the diet.

What is more, this increase in meat and poultry production per capita across a hundred years took place against a background of nearly doubled populations. Of course, much of the increase was sustained by imports from abroad (for instance, more than half our bacon and nearly half our mutton and lamb, contributing to the daily £2 million that we spend on imported meat); but intensification remains the crucial story about British agriculture.

Most vegetarian or animal welfare campaigners now stress that at the very least the population ought to break its overwhelming dependence on meat as a source of dietary protein. Not less than 40 to 60 per cent of protein eaten in the West comes from animal products (Food Standards Committee, *Report on Novel Protein Foods*, HMSO, 1974). Alan Long puts the figure as nearer 62 per cent in Britain and around 80 per cent in America. He and other campaigners insist over and over again that:

1. modern animal husbandry involves many practices which are miserable for animals and potentially dangerous for man;

2. we do not need animal products for health; and

3. our agriculture is badly distorted by the present need to feed so many animals, which are very poor converters of plant protein into meat protein.

They would like to see a reverse in the trend of thousands of years.

A thousand years before Christ became that Good Shepherd to His flock, the people of the British Iron Age were keeping domestic animals in some form or other in their settlements. Their sheep and pigs were practically wild, and if their nearest modern equivalents (Soay sheep, cross-bred European wild boar and the Tamworth pig) are anything to go by, they were rangy, long-legged athletes who could outrun and outjump humans and dogs. Hunting and domestication probably went side by side, and were often synonymous. There is evidence that goats, geese, hens and ducks were all kept in some form. Fish were often reared in ponds, and oysters in special beds.

By the beginning of the nineteenth century, 80 per cent of the labour force still worked directly in agriculture. Later, industrialization was as much predicated on the ability of fewer farmers to feed more people as it was upon there being new things to make and new ways of making them. But of course, industrialization also depended on huge numbers of the population being herded from very often appalling privation in the country to yet worse privation in the cities.

There never was an age of rural bliss and plenty, but it is likely that the pre-Victorian peasant had some chance of at least a share in a household pig and in a poached fish or bird. The nineteenth century decreed that the peasant's farmer-employer no longer had charge of his board; and when he was also deprived of land of his own, his diet declined almost as dramatically, it appears, as did that of his relatives who went to the city in search of work. The evacuation of the countryside has never stopped. By the 1970s there were around a million people directly employed in agriculture (though each 'supports' several more in agriculture's service and industrial ancilliaries); many of these are part-time or casual.

The table on page 34 can tell only some of the story: it gives the figures for certain species of farm animals for two years across the last and the present centuries. But it disguises the relationship between the number of human attendants and their animals. It is also anachronistic in two other respects: the early agricultural reports tell us that about 2 million horses were on the land at the end of the nineteenth century (up by a half since the mid-century); and chickens are not mentioned at all, being merely a sideline.

Populations of UK farm animals (in thousands)

	Cattle	Sheep	Pigs
1831	5,220	39,650	4,000
1981	13,209	32,282	7,853

Sources: *Chambers Encyclopaedia*, 1904; House of Commons Agriculture Committee, *Animal Welfare in Poultry, Pig and Veal Calf Production. Volume One: Report, Proceedings of the Committee and Appendices; Volume Two: Minutes of Evidence*, HMSO, 1981.

Intensification

Nobody a hundred years ago seems to have bothered to have commented upon the contribution to the population's diet rendered by chicken meat. By the first and second decades of the twentieth century, it was noted that the consumption was about five pounds per capita per annum of poultry and game. Consumption had doubled by the time of, and was interrupted by, the Second World War, when it fell back to 1913 levels. It slowly rose to around twelve pounds per head by 1960. It doubled again to twenty-four pounds by 1970, and has kept rising since. In a hundred years it has at least quintupled. And while consumption of poultry and game has rocketed (and egg consumption has risen threefold in the period), the disappearance of the farmyard hen also occurred.

The poultry trade is one long saga of increasing egg production from the hen population, and of the creation of a new kind of lifestyle for broiler birds – currently 58 million of them – in which they would never lay an egg or see the light of day except in one blinding trip in a lorry to the slaughter. The poultry-meat trade, once mostly consisting in what few old layers the farm hands did not eat, has been revolutionized. Old layers now go to pets and pies, or end up in baby-foods and tinned vichys-soise. The story of the battery hen and the deep-litter broiler is especially worth telling because it is among the most extreme of the intensifications which have taken place. It has brought into our slaughterhouses a creature which previously would have scratched out its life on the farmyard and only been culled at the end of a long and presumably 'natural' life. It has taken the creature that we interfered with least and turned it into the one that we interfere with most.

The four crucial principles of intensification are also shown clearly in the poultry trade for meat or eggs. Firstly, the farmer prefers that the food be taken to the animal rather than gathered by the animal itself. Secondly, the farmer prefers the animal's environment to be strictly controlled. Thirdly, the health of an individual animal is not paramount if the productivity of the flock is maintained. Fourthly, it is usually a good intensive principle to remove the baby from the mother as early as poss-ible – we are more potent feeders of baby animals than their mothers are.

Intensification is only the final solution to the problem of domestication, which has always meant the gradually increased confinement of animals. Their feeding habits could be controlled by the farmer to a greater degree: they could eat more of what the farmer chose to give them instead of what they could graze or peck for themselves. But also they could be improved as energy converters. It now takes only seven weeks to get a chicken to a weight of around four pounds. In the forties, that would have taken more than thirteen weeks. A cock turkey, one of the country's 15 or so million intensively raised turkeys, reaches sixteen pounds in sixteen weeks.

The farmer is part ecologist and part economist: he must regulate the energy flows on his farm so that they produce the best economic flows available to him. An animal that walks about in search of food is using much of its energy in locomo-tion. This is energy which is wasted from the farmer's point of view. He would rather that the creature stayed put and let its energy go into flesh. But locomotion is also bad from a farmer's point of view because it makes the animal fit and strong – its meat becomes tough and stringy (though, arguably, more tasty). He does not need a fit animal, he only needs one that is not diseased, or whose diseases can be mass-dosed into submission. Sometimes the process goes too far, even for the farmer: turkeys (now mostly produced in the broiler system) have now been bred so fat that they cannot support themselves on their underdeveloped legs; and because this has proved counterproductive, they are now being bred with sturdier legs.

According to John Weller's *History of the Farmstead*, the origin of the intensive poultry systems was the British Electrical Development Association's promotion of the virtues of using artificial heat about the farm, and using it on animals, in the twenties. By 1932, there was a handbook, *Electricity in Poultry Farming*, which promoted the notion of 'outdoor foster mothers'. These were heated boards which could be used to 'foster' hundreds of chicks at a time. One farmer was raising motherless chicks in batches of 2,000 at a time. By the 1950s there was an embarrassing surplus of grain in the rich world, and intensively kept animals seemed a sensible way of profitably consuming it.

This is where the sums become complicated and where the industrialization of farming comes into its own. The farmyard hen lived a full life and scratched about for her food. She might have had a few grains here and there from the farmer's corn supply, and scraps from the kitchen table. Her eggs were a handy and small supplement to the farmer's income. This is called low-input, low-output farming, and in fact her well-being and that of the farmer were in far healthier balance than is the case now. The hen running with the other animals on a farm is actually a very efficient and useful contributor to the overall commercial ecosystem: she is a scourge to many of the pests and parasites on the bigger animals.

Among the most serious effects of intensive farming is the recent phenomenon whereby the individual animal's welfare is worth sacrificing for the profitability of the flock or herd. It is worth risking the loss of a percentage of animals through overcrowding, or a small loss of weight in all of them, if the flock as a whole is doing better commercially from intensification. This is very like the 'tragedy of the commons', identified by Professor Garrett Hardin, who postulated that common land had a chronic tendency to overgrazing, since it would always seem to be in the personal interests of any individual commoner to add one more animal to his herd, even if it inevitably meant that the well-being of the village's land was reduced by the action. Whether this is historically true or not does not matter: it is a model of the phenomenon which is certainly true of factory farming. Add one more hen to a flock of ten, and even if each does marginally less well – or suffers more – the equation is still profitable. Only in factory farming is it the animals alone that suffer. As the *Farmer's Weekly* (17 September 1982) commented:

Today, rising standards of living have led to many veterinary surgeons concentrating on domestic animals – be they dog, cat, horse or hamster. Many veterinarians find this more satisfying than farm practice, in that often they act in the best interests of the animal rather than be influenced by agricultural economics.

Alan Long has computed that vets on average spend about 27 per cent of their time on farm animals, which outnumber pets by about ten to one.

Moreover, even if it was not the case that it is not crucial that each animal thrives provided that the overall flock is profitable, it is certainly not true, as the industry is inclined to say, that animals do not thrive if they are not well. The National Farmers' Union calls it a 'very well-known and accepted fact' that animals only do well if they are fit, in spite of evidence that many animals will support quite severe injuries and still put on weight. And few people suggest that battery or broiler birds are strong and fit; but they do perform adequately.

Furthermore, before the House of Commons Agriculture Committee investigation in 1980 and 1981 (*Animal Welfare in Poultry, Pig and Veal Calf Production*), the National Farmers' Union tried to perpetrate a further classic nonsense. They reproduced a controversial paper suggesting that animals adapt to battery conditions. The idea is that animals can be made genetically and habitually 'natural' battery creatures, happier in batteries than out. Actually, the most that can be done is to develop creatures that have a genetically acquired tendency to calmness in captivity. This does not at all mean that their capacity to revert right back to and to prefer their natural behaviour has been subverted, as has been proved time and time again. Chickens taken from battery farms very quickly grow their feathers again (where they have lost them, and not all do), begin to scratch and peck, and become – after an initial period of stunned disorientation – the thorough-going hen.

The modern farmer is not raising individual animals for sale and slaughter: he is raising herds and flocks. He is dealing with huge numbers of animals with a small net profit on each, but large sums of money involved in total. It becomes important to count every penny. Hens, for instance, convert plant-food energy into 'egg energy' at a ratio of about twenty to one, and in battery systems they need in addition about thirteen units of fossil-fuel energy for every unit of food energy they produce. Luckily for the farmers, they convert the money invested in feed and heat into profit from sales rather more efficiently. By the sixties, in response to rising food prices, it became well worthwhile to make the chickens convert their food energy more efficiently; and it didn't matter if their fossil-energy price went up somewhat in the process, because food constitutes about 70 per cent of an intensively kept chicken's cost.

Visit one of Christopher Turton's chicken houses in Sussex, and you can see the result in the case of the broiler hen destined for the table. On his farm he has two long, low, wooden sheds. There are no windows. In the vestibule is a control panel, with which Christopher Turton can manage the light, heat and food inputs into the shed. 'The aim,' he says, 'is thermo-neutrality. We want the houses at the temperature where the birds aren't using much energy to keep warm in winter or cool in summer.'

At first the sight is hard to believe. Under the roof light-bulbs glow, rather dimly. Great fans in the walls of the interior are sucking out air constantly on a summer day. And the floor, as large as an aircraft hanger, is carpeted in white-feathered birds. At the end of their 51-day growing period they are of a size which means that 25,000 birds fill the floor space. They could walk about and stretch their wings if they wanted, but mostly seem to sit quite quietly or just stretch their legs periodically in a mildly curious exploration of their surroundings. One or two are beak-agape and appear to be gasping.

But the overall air is of quiet, plump, well-feathered birds, living the dreary lives of prisoners everywhere, who have grown accustomed to their confinement or never knew anything else. They do not panic when one walks among them (though it is embarrassing to do so, as if one ought not to display ordinary curiosity – rather as royalty must feel when being shown round a factory of machinists). They live on a litter of sawdust which was clean and pink when delivered and is now a dry, dunged, brown dust. But it is not noisome stuff; it is rather like humus or dried peat. The air is fairly sweet to the nose and clean to the throat: any damp would make the accumulated droppings hideously ammoniac.

Chris Turton makes his ninety-acre farm work hard for him. He is shrewd and knows how to squeeze profit from his capital, as anyone must. But he is a man with a balanced view of life. He does not strike one as someone who would throw moral scruples out of the window in order to become rich (and he does not expect to become rich). More than this, he is prepared to lay himself open to discussion, even with severe critics. To which end, a few days before he showed me his farm, he had been in London discussing factory farming at the Institute of Contemporary Arts' 1981 summer series of seminars on animals and their rights. And so it is he who points out what one would not see at a casual inspection.

We lose about 6 to 10 per cent of our birds. These intensively raised animals have no constitutions, you know. Sometimes they just seem to get heart failure because of the strain imposed by terrific growth rates. And often their legs or backs seem to give out: they grow so fast that their bone structure cannot keep up with them.

Chris Turton believes that the current overstocking – defined as any stocking density in which the individual animal does less well than it might – is now a financial necessity whose advantages are passed on to the consumer. He accepts that people who keep animals in modern systems may well become

desensitized to their plight, but rebuts charges of deliberate
cruelty. He is far from mealy-mouthed on the subject, as a
duplicated sheet which constant inquiries have led him to produce says (though he seems to have fallen victim to some of the
National Farmers' Union line):

There is little, if any, evidence of outright cruelty to animals kept
intensively, and there is a good reason for this: they simply would not
thrive, and the narrow profit margin on which the system operates
would soon turn to loss. However, this does not mean that all the
animals are perfectly happy, for their close confinement brings some
degree of both physical and mental stress upon them, and it is probably
true to say that the freedoms they gain, from hunger, from thirst, from
cold, from fear, do not make up for those which they have lost.

His hens do not experience, he says, the famous 'vices' or
behavioural quirks – usually violent – which are supposed to
occur in broiler-farmed birds. His birds keep their beaks intact,
while many battery hens have theirs cropped in an operation
which is very painful unless carried out with extreme care and
which some chicken farmers perform in order to stop birds
pecking at one another. Nor have his hens ever experienced the
mass panic which has been known suddenly to overtake a flock
and which can lead to deaths as the entire population of a
broiler house tries to crowd into one corner, heap upon heap.

Chris Turton knows the dangerous stages in the development of his mono-aged flock.

Three weeks in can be a difficult time. We can keep the light low then,
but if it is too low they won't bother to eat. If it is too high, it can lead to
feather-pecking and ultimately to cannibalism. Our whole object is to
get them to eat as much as we possibly can and keep any form of stress
away from them.

The question does not arise for him as to whether he might do
with a less intensive system and give the birds a more natural
life. 'This system is profitable if we have 25,000 birds in each
house, but not if we have 20,000 in each.'

It was disease control which most held up the progress of
intensification. Like any monoculture, whether plant or animal,
intensive husbandry uses breeds which have been developed

for productivity but may be short of stamina, which, combined with the kind of confinement which is ideal for contagion, makes tightly packed animals very susceptible to infection. Intensive husbandry has thus led to a worrying increase in the amount of automatic medication – 'medication on tap' as one advertiser branded it. Some of this tries to improve on natural growth-rates; some growth-promoting hormones – whether real or synthetic – are still allowed to be used by farmers without any reference to vets. And antibiotics are used routinely, both on and off prescription by vets, though some are safeguarded in case any animal immunization is passed on to humans.

Some of the feeds which Christopher Turton uses for his flocks are medicated, but they must be withdrawn from the birds some days before slaughter in order to eliminate danger to humans. Otherwise, the birds in the deep-litter house have an endless supply of food, which is shunted round in thin troughs on a conveyor belt. A lorry comes regularly from the company which owns the birds and the food, and which to that extent capitalizes Chris Turton's operations and under which he becomes a kind of franchiser. The margins of his profitability are charted out: the number of birds that he is given at the beginning of each of the year's five 'crops'; the strain of bird; and the sort of food he will be getting. He can order up more food whenever he wants, which arrives in a tanker and is augered up into gravity feed silos.

For every 215 tons of food fed to his chickens, Chris Turton needs to see 100 tons of chicken meat to be profitable. If he needs 230 tons to get 100 tons of chickens, he has failed, he says. And so, at the end of the process, each of his two flocks of birds are gobbling up 3 tons of food a day. Each of his bird houses uses 1,000 gallons of water a day; some of it goes through the chickens down into the deep litter, and the rest is blown out through the fans as vapour.

The British Electrical Development Association would be proud of him: his electricity bill for the farm is £350 a month, and that does not include the heating for the sheds – done by gas, at £6,000 a year.

Chris Turton is one of about 2,000 farmers who are engaged in keeping broilers in the UK. His flock is twice the size of the average poultry farmer's 22,000 or so. But well over half of the country's broilers are kept in flocks of 100,000 or more. The course of this intensification looks smooth. *The Changing Structure of Agriculture 1968–1975* (HMSO), a government report published in 1977, found that between 1968 and 1975 the number of broilers went up from 33·6 million to 47·4 million (an increase of 40 per cent). But the numbers of producers plummets periodically and traumatically: intensive farming is an unstable way of making a fortune. Between 1968 and 1969 a third of the producers went out of business, and between 1973 and 1975 a further quarter of the producers went out. Demand throughout the period fluctuated, but overall increased slightly.

Indeed, Chris Turton has seen one of the most dramatic upheavals. He used to be allied to a smallish firm, which was bought up by Imperial Tobacco, which became an immense owner of broiler operations. But they lost £10 million in their brief excursion. Now the industry has regrouped around smaller main owners.

Whatever one thinks of the broiler-house production of chickens, it is regarded as one of the few factory-farming methods which does not pose welfare problems for animals – that at least is the view of the respected and diligent House of Commons Agriculture Committee, whose report is an authoritative account of the modern factory-farming debate. 'The raising of broiler chickens ... was little mentioned in evidence,' they declared.

The raising of battery hens for eggs is, on the other hand, the source of constant controversy. Roughly speaking, the current system involves three, four or even six tiered banks of cages in which usually five (but sometimes four or six) birds live in a cage 50 × 45 centimetres (the larger of which measurements is about the distance from an adult man's shoulder to his wrist). This is regarded as a grotesquely cruel way of keeping birds by almost all who see it. It is a system which is supposed to avoid some of the behavioural problems associated with anything less than the most free-range chicken-keeping. Even in the happiest *natural!*

farmyard, there sometimes arises a runt chicken who can be bullied to death by the others. In more confined chicken-keeping systems, the problems of cannibalism and bullying can be endemic. Apologists say that they are somewhat reduced in battery systems, at least as compared with confined and poorly run non-cage intensive systems.

The Commons Committee admitted that the birds which they saw in one, probably model, though certainly intensive, system 'looked healthy and sounded contented'. But they had heard evidence that scientists have come – with that typical, cruelly slow precision of judgement of theirs – to the view that animals have behavioural as well as physical needs. It is clear that a battery cage does not allow anything like the expression of behavioural needs. Worse perhaps, there is good evidence that battery birds are very fragile skeletally. And there have been many accounts of birds whose claws have grown round the wire of their cages, and of a high incidence of baldness because of the wear and tear of living in wire cages.

In 1965, the Brambell Committee had decided that animals at the least ought to be accorded the basic freedom to stretch their legs and wings, to turn round, to lie down and to groom themselves, and the Agriculture Committee allowed this view to be strengthened by evidence which they heard such as that from Dr Barry Hughes, to the effect that 'welfare on a general level is a state of complete mental and physical health, where the animal is in harmony with its environment'. But fine words butter no parsnips!

Stocking densities lead to complicated sums: five or six birds to a cage is said not to be ideally productive, partly because of increased cannibalism, but the overall results from the increased numbers are said to be economically worthwhile. However, some evidence was given to the Committee that suggested that lower densities might be managed to produce higher productivity. The government quango, the Farm Animal Welfare Council, has recommended an increase in the area of cage per bird.

Compassion in World Farming (CIWF) have always had their best success campaigning against the battery egg: in

March 1982, for instance, they began sending the Queen two free-range eggs a day, intended, reported the *Times* diarist, for her breakfast. Peter Roberts, CIWF's secretary, said, 'It is incredible that with 4,000 acres of royal farms they are unable to supply her with non-battery eggs.' The eggs which Roberts started to send came from Bedales School, where Princess Margaret's daughter, Lady Sarah Armstrong-Jones, is a pupil. The gift was CIWF's response to the news that a royal warrant had been awarded to a firm which makes regular deliveries of battery eggs to Buckingham Palace.

But Her Majesty gets her free-range eggs free – would humbler Britons stump up extra for the humane egg? There is some evidence that a considerable minority of the public will pay more for an egg which they feel is humanely produced. The Free Range Egg Association (FREGG) operates an endorsement scheme. Approved producers do not actually have to operate free-range husbandry in the (fairly) strict 150-birds-to-the-acre definition, but must certainly give their birds at the very least two square feet of shed *and* access to the open air. Shops which are acknowledged as selling FREGG-approved eggs can display the FREGG sign – a hen with her egg in a triangle.

The hero of the better egg is Martin Pitt, of Wiltshire. 'Mr Pitt's hens are plump, glossy, inquisitive and sweet-smelling,' crooned the *Observer* (26 July 1981) after a visit. The Commons Committee appear not to have been aware of Mr Pitt's aviary system, in which sheds house 1,800 hens each. The birds lay in traditional nesting boxes and have access both to an outside enclosure and to the rest of their hen house. As the *Observer* said:

In the eyes of the conventional farming community, Mr Pitt has achieved the impossible. Put those numbers of hens together, walking about and pecking in their own droppings, he was told, and you'll lose them all through disease and cannibalism. Perch them in tiered perches and they'll defecate on one another.

However, it appears that Martin Pitt is under no illusions that his system will sweep the board: the eggs cost more (£1·20 per dozen in the summer of 1981), and the degree of work that the chickens require would rule the system out for most people.

Intensive production, money and pollution

It is just possible, as the Commons Committee recognized, that systems which require rather more work, and therefore create more jobs, than others (and perhaps bring a saving in energy or feed costs) may soon be regarded in a better light than they are now, when we are still in the sway of the 'white heat of technology' mentality so beloved of politicians of all stamps twenty years ago.

Their report actually framed as one of its recommendations what must be one of the first revisions of established, received opinion and conventional wisdom on the nature of productivity. As such, it is well worth stating here:

> For the time being we make no specific recommendation on taxation policy except to invite the Minister, in consultation where necessary with his Treasury colleagues, to keep this possible aspect of financial policy in mind and try, on the one hand, to avoid measures which will encourage the trend to undesirable methods and, on the other, to see whether incentives can be devised . . . to encourage more humane ones, taking into account the possibility that in today's circumstances less dependence on energy and more on labour may on both counts have considerable advantages.

'Today's circumstances' may be taken to mean high energy prices and the three and a half million unemployed.

The business of taxation and subsidy is very important in agriculture. The farmers' grip on the public imagination and purse is considerable. It has led to a system in which they are paid good prices for their produce, often whether the consumer wants it or not, and to a system of subsidy which, described briefly, encourages farmers to buy machinery and sack employees. Moreover, farming does not attract rates, so, though it can be a powerful nuisance, it pays little towards the cleaning-up process.

Richard Body, barrister, MP on the Commons Agriculture

Committee and a farmer, repeatedly referred to the tax advantages donated towards intensification. He asked the RSPCA why they did not press for a change in the tax position of intensive farmers:

If I keep my dry sows, as I would prefer to, in a field, I get no grants, no tax allowances; on the contrary, I have to buy or rent some land; the only grant I get is a fencing grant of 25 per cent and that is discretionary – I know of no pig producer who has succeeded in getting a grant for that . . . However, if I keep my sows in sow stalls, it may cost many thousands of pounds to put up a suitable building. Have you calculated the enormous tax advantage there is available if I go to sow stalls; and if you have done so, would you not agree that it tilts the balance very unfairly in favour of those who go into an intensive system and very unfairly against those who rather keep their sows in fields, using up poor-quality land and using other methods we used to prefer in days gone by?

The modern pig industry was a creation of the post-war desire to be finished with rationing. The pig had been a small-time farmer's animal before the war. Until the practice was forbidden by planning regulations, many were kept by miners in the north-east. The backyard pig was a familiar animal, as it still is on the Continent, especially in the country. But among the formal suppliers of the pig-meat market, the numbers were reduced to nearly a tenth in the twenty years after the war, from 200,000 to 30,000. However, in that time the pig herd hugely increased (between 1947 and 1954, the pig population went from 1·6 million to 6·3 million).

Beyond their general enthusiasm to tax-aid expensive intensification of farming, governments have periodically gone out of their way to encourage pig production. A phenomenon developed in which the population and profitability of pigs fluctuated wildly in response to the government's every variation – and they were frequent – in subsidy towards pig-keeping. Pig-keeping is something which can be gone in for very quickly, and just as quickly be got out of. It is the ideal opportunist farming.

There was concern in the Commons Committee that government-funded research was too often about productivity and not often enough about welfare, and it was too often into intensification rather than into making old methods more profitable. As Richard Body asked the RSPCA witnesses:

Given the undoubted fact that there must be millions of tax-payers in this country who are concerned about intensive forms of production, and who really don't care for it, is it really right in those circumstances that so much public money should be devoted to ever more research into more intensive forms of animal production?

The pig is a much exploited animal, but also a complicated one. It produces many offspring, but with quite long baby-rearing. A period of 115 days of pregnancy is followed by fifty-six days of suckling. A 20 per cent mortality rate of young piglets is not uncommon in the first few days and 50 per cent of deaths of piglets are perinatal: the mother pig is notoriously prone to crushing her young and is nowadays restrained in a farrowing crate (in which she can be bodily turned on her side or made to stand up) or tethered to the ground during the crucial period after the birth of her young.

In common with all intensive farming, the practice has been to attempt to wean the young earlier and earlier, especially so that the sow can be made pregnant again, which is increasingly done by artificial insemination. There have been officially funded experiments into weaning piglets at one day old. The Ministry of Agriculture told the House of Commons Agriculture Committee that fifty-six weeks was the weaning age for the bulk of pig farmers now, but that 40 per cent weaned their piglets at less than four weeks. Some do it at ten days. Many are settling now for three weeks' weaning. Luckily for them, piglets appear to do badly if weaned younger than this, and the practice has not caught on, though there has been a sinister development: piglets are sometimes now delivered by hysterectomy from five-year-old sows who would otherwise be at risk of throwing stillbirths. The mother is then immediately slaughtered.

Chris Turton's piglets, like most, go into a sweat-box at the age of three weeks and stay there for thirty days. A sweat-box is small, ill lit and bleak; it is not, however, as peculiarly horrid as its name implies. At least, it is not noticeably worse than, for instance, the monopitch sheds in which the pigs go for the remainder of their short (five to six months) lives. Nevertheless, Chris Turton now regrets building the sweat-boxes.

In common with most intensively kept animals, pigs are prone to diseases whose effect is made much worse by the close confinement of large numbers of animals. Each pig unit now contains a higher percentage of the huge national pig herd than was the case even ten or twenty years before. Both swine vesicular disease (SVD) and Aujeszky's disease are common problems in the UK herd; together with foot-and-mouth disease, which has identical presenting symptoms and occasionally assails our animals, the only solution to SVD and Aujeszky's disease is wholesale slaughtering of affected populations. The swine vesicular virus often lives in infected food, and enters the animal's system through any abrasions that it can find, and the problem is that many restless pigs on factory farms bruise and eventually cut themselves in their stalls as they go through the motions of rooting around and scratching, trying to make a wooded-landscape habitat out of their prisons. Aujeszky's disease is not yet common, but it is spreading. Both diseases are typical corollaries of intensive methods and poor husbandry. SVD entered the scene a decade ago and is controlled by compulsory slaughtering, which has already cost £12 million.

Pigs are also prone to wear away patches on their shoulders and elbows as they try to make themselves comfortable on bare concrete floors in their sheds. Bedding is usually a luxury that pigs have to do without. They may not enjoy bleeding from their shoulders; but until they cease to thrive or at least lose profitability, they have to live with it, in spite of the discomfort.

Pigs are notorious for sudden, inexplicable outbreaks of violence (which advocates of free-range pig farming say hardly ever occur outside intensive systems), and occasionally savage one another. The habit of tail-docking (in which, in the best practice, a few inches of the pigs' tails are removed as near as possible to birth) is necessary because pigs sometimes begin to eat one another's tail-ends: there is no feeling in the tip of a pig's tail and blood can be drawn without the victim realizing the event. The aggressor becomes incensed by the sight of blood, and more serious damage ensues.

A greater problem from the factory farmer's point of view is that of stress at slaughter. Cattle and pigs, but especially pigs, are inclined to produce poor meat because of the stress and exhaustion involved with being carted to the slaughterhouse. The Meat Research Institute has been working on ways of detecting meat which is likely to be affected rather quickly.

Pre-slaughter stress makes some animals produce post-mortem acid in their muscles at accelerated and increased rates which, in combination with warmth in the slaughterhouses, produces in pigs a quality in their meat which is known as PSE (pale, soft and exudative). This means that the meat is colourless, squidgy when cut, and sweats. Anywhere between one in five and one in ten of pigs are affected. Some pigs are genetically rather poor performers in this respect: the long, lean Pietrain pig is especially difficult. It has few piglets (a disadvantage) and is prone to stress (another disadvantage); but against these problems the breeder can balance its lean meat and miserly dietary habits (it may eat 20 to 25 per cent less than other breeds).

As usual in the curiously depraved world of animal exploitation, the problem of PSE meat is seen as one for the consumer and the farmer. The unfortunate fact that animals suffer dramatic hormonological changes due to the misery and shock of their last few hours is not regarded as something which ought to worry us from their point of view.

The business of pig production takes no account of what pigs might conceivably want. With fierce competition and high capital costs, the profit margin is constantly squeezed. The factory farmer is in a position to make large sums of money, but he is also under the typical modern pressure of having to finance expensive loan capital in order to keep up with the intensification in which other farmers are also engaging. The equation is one in which cheap food for the consumer is achieved by putting higher and higher quantities of capital to work with ever increasing stock densities of animals. In many cases it is worth spending money on high-cost houses for animals, provided that the cost of the installation is offset by the increased densities that can be achieved while not incurring proportionate costs in feed (the animals move less, use less food and increase their own contribution to the heat of the building).

Meat is no longer a means of storing protein on the hoof for the seasons when the vegetable kingdom cannot provide food. It is no longer a marginal product produced on marginal land. The primitive farmer sees animals as useful for cultivating his land: they provide haulage; in the case of pigs they work virtually as ploughs; they fertilize the land; they use otherwise wasted food. Contrariwise, intensive production has environmental hazards rather than advantages. Its energy intensification binds us closely to dangerous power systems. Around three times as much energy is used to feed one person in the UK as is available to a person in a 'developing' country for all purposes.

British slaughterhouses produce a tide of blood, about 24 million gallons every year, of which little is used. Animals produce around 170 million tons of undiluted excreta in Britain every year, of which 60 million tons is produced by animals in sheds. It is hardly ever where it is wanted, and constitutes a deepening problem. On Humberside, where the pig industry is concentrated, the crisis has led to the local authorities formulating special planning regulations about the distance between intensive farms and the maximum slurry disposal per hectare to be allowed in future. (Meanwhile, many farmers are surprised to discover that they are, under the present government, freer than ever to build pig units without planning permission.)

In 1979 the Royal Commission on Environmental Pollution's seventh report, *Agriculture and Pollution* (HMSO, Cmnd 7644), expressed particular concern about the poor treatment given to animal waste in slurry tanks. But it was also concerned that too much human raw sewage was still dumped on Britain's fields, and that this was a potent source of infection, especially of salmonella (which kills tens of people every year), through the widespread abuse of the best advice that six months must elapse from application of raw sewage to a field with animals grazing there. The Commission's anxieties were expressed in

1979, and nothing has been done since then to improve the position.

Other sorts of problem arise with large numbers of animals in modern agriculture: for instance, 63,000 tonnes of sheep-dip chemicals must be disposed of every year.

It may be that these dangers to the public will do more than the sufferings of animals to bring about a revulsion for intensive methods. The cheapskate environmental habits which factory farming has brought about may well yet produce an epidemic of disease which will make the mucky old farmyard of yesteryear appear as it actually was: a place where at least dung was properly sterilized by fermentation (in ancient Turkey, newly eunuched palace guards were left standing in muck to sterilize their wounds), something which rarely happens in the relative cool of concrete slurry tanks for all their look of modernity.

When Ruth Harrison used the expression 'animal machine' for farm animals as the title of her campaigning (which set off an enormous controversy and led to the Brambell Committee), she was precisely marking the development of a different role for animals. They were no longer ancillary to farming; it no longer mattered that an animal can convert only around 10 per cent of its feed into something useful for humans, since Western society was now concerned more with luxury than with sustenance agriculture. The factory farm is really a way of minimizing the inconvenience which Creation has built into animals as a means of feeding people. It is specifically designed to override the animal's biological needs wherever they compete with our demands upon it.

The scientists tell us that we cannot strictly be sure what the needs of a pig are. They cannot deny that we know a good deal about their last hours, since the stress they feel then has tangible results which are costly to us (PSE meat cost the industry around £750,000 in 1977). But actually a good deal can be surmised. They do not like to be overcrowded, and indeed Christopher Turton finds that reducing the normal and advised densities of pig has productivity benefits. Several pig farmers are now returning to old-fashioned, free-range pig-keeping as a solution to the problems of disease, feed, energy costs and consciences. When animals were kept on poor land, and when most land was what we would now call marginal, these things could be managed rather differently. Part of the medieval pattern of countryside use had forests, woods and scrub as grazing land. Much of this might quite have suited pigs and what we know of their 'natural' needs.

The farm animal myth

The notion that moral decisions about food might become very important is not absurd. Research done by the environmental group Earth Resources Research suggests that up to 40 per cent of people would pay more for humanely produced eggs. And when Sir William Elliott, chairman of the House of Commons Agriculture Committee, says, having seen veal production by the notorious crate method, that he could not eat veal again, he is only one of thousands who have in effect revolutionized veal production in this country by voting with their boycotting power. Some butchers will not even sell it.

But serious moves to highlight the role of conscience will be combated by the farming industry and the National Farmers' Union in particular, and their governmental henchmen inside the Ministry of Agriculture, Fisheries and Food (MAFF). Already we have the milk industry sponsoring the advertising slogan for cream – 'Naughty But Nice' – with what must be unintentional irony.

In supermarkets and market stalls, eggs which have come from battery hens and been packed automatically into boxes are carefully taken out and redisplayed in 'traditional' wicker baskets with a little straw, the imagined bedding of the imaginary contented bird which might have laid them years ago but certainly hardly ever exists now. The hen of old of course knew cold winters and wet nights – there is no real rural idyll, past or present. Compassion in World Farming, a campaigning group, have drawn attention to French prosecutions of farmers who used too glowing a description of their farming in their packaging. However, the dairy industry represents the myth-machine at its most powerful. Daisy the cow is the archetype of contentment; 'cow-like' is the very epitome of complacency. The cow is still seen as grazing in the field, even if the hen and the pig have been banished into factory sheds.

But it was the cow which Alan Long tried to defend in a typically stalwart letter to *The Times* in June 1981. In it he noted that:

The obsession with protein, particularly of animal origin, and the greed for 'convenient' and 'cheap' food (with the consequent unwillingness to pay for decent work and stockmanship on the farm) have contributed to the development of a mechanized 'aggroculture', stuffing feed into animals remarkable for their output and fecundity, short gestation and rapid growth before puberty ...

Although pigs and poultry have been notoriously exploited, the cow too has suffered. Shakespeare used the plight of the cow and her calf to illustrate a paradigm of man's remorselessness. Four centuries later mankind goes to even greater lengths to squeeze milk and calves out of her.

In the last twenty-five years yields of milk from the cow have been increased by a third, while the time spent in direct stockmanship has been reduced from 123 to 44 hours per year per cow. Mastitis (a catarrh-like discharge into the milk in the udder) constantly threatens the British herd. Profligate medication cannot save the modern cow from culling due to 'overproduction' diseases before she can start her fourth lactation.

There was some more in this vein. A week later came the riposte. A Somerset farmer of thirty-five years' experience wrote that he had read Long's charges with 'anger and indignation'.

The increase in yields has been made possible by the increase in knowledge of a great many people. The manufacturers of cattle cake who produce a better article; the plant breeders who have bred more productive strains of grasses and clovers; the veterinary surgeons who have a greater understanding of the needs of a dairy cow; and perhaps even those of us who breed cattle can take a little credit.

Mastitis is certainly an ever present problem, but in our herd it is less of a problem than it was thirty years ago, and I would think this is generally the case. To suggest that it 'constantly threatens the British herd' is to overdramatize the position. Does the common cold constantly threaten the British people?

High yields neither shorten the lives nor worsen the health of dairy cows. [He notes in a letter commenting on this chapter that mastitis is not in any case an 'overproduction' disease, but is usually caused by draughts.] So-called 'overproduction' diseases are nearly always caused by underfeeding or incorrect feeding. In our herd of seventy cows, we have three now milking well in their eleventh lactation and in calf again; all three have been high yielders throughout their lives.

My son and I run a typical family farm and do all the milking ourselves, and therefore represent the majority of dairy farmers in this country. We take a simple pride and pleasure in the high production of our cows, and in their health and general well-being. To suggest that we are exploiting them is untrue and unjust.

May I take this opportunity of inviting Dr Long to leave the make-believe world of Kensington, and savour the realities of life on a dairy farm in Somerset. We should be pleased to welcome him and any member of his society.

Alan Long and I (reporting for *The Times*) duly went to Somerset to meet the farmer, Jim Morrish. His cows were, to all appearances, the perfect image of good health. Sturdy beige Jerseys who came muzzling up to the two debaters in their yard, they glowed in the afternoon sun. The difficulty is that they are not able to say, one way or another, whether or not they enjoy having the immense and genetically contrived udders (Jim Morrish stresses that much good work has been done on udder conformation recently) which produce between five and six gallons of milk a day, or something like four stones of milk from an udder originally designed to feed one calf. And of course the cow cannot tell us what she feels every year as her calf is stolen from her almost at birth. Anyone who hears their lowing – it is called 'belving' – at this time is bound to be moved, though the awful noise seldom lasts long, and some fairly brutal butchering goes on in the world. But just as there is evidence that many animals can be alarmed (measured by hormonological changes and heart-beat) without displaying any outward distress, so cows may well be far less 'content' than they look.

'I enjoy my cows and I enjoy looking after them,' said Jim Morrish, and he seemed perhaps a little mournful of the pressures that farmers are under to improve production of their farms at the cost of people's jobs and a good deal of tradition, though he did not regret the passing of the days when, without medication available, cows in herds thirty years ago sometimes had udders and teats so rotten that the latter might come away in the hand of the milker. When he began farming, his 160 acres supported forty cows and five men; now his seventy cows are already proving unproductive and he is considering increasing his herd to eighty-five. The pattern of his herd size follows that of others: nationally, the average dairy herd size increased by between 6 and 8 per cent per year from 1968 until the mid-seventies at least. In 1969 the average dairy herd was twenty-one; in 1975 it was thirty, with more than a quarter in herds over one hundred.

Jim Morrish says that he is very careful about the use of antibiotics with his animals, and he certainly would not agree that he is the Pharmacist Giles of Alan Long's famously phrased castigation. He said he had had only a couple of clinical cases of mastitis in the past few months and that only for these would he have used antibiotics. Nevertheless, cows are routinely dosed with antibiotics. 17 million antibiotic shots are injected annually up the teats of British herds, when the cows are being dried off preparatory to a new insemination and pregnancy or during lactation.

There have been many accusations that the beef and dairy business is heavily dependent on drugs. Growth-promoting hormones which have been suspected of causing damage to humans have been routinely used on farm animals for years – though the British have introduced some controls this year – as have been low but continuous doses of antibiotics. (In the case of calves, growth-promoting pellets are inserted behind the calves' ears, so as to avoid tainting; the process obviously alarms them.) Many farmers do strongly disapprove of modern drug practices and do resist them. Others, of course, are less scrupulous. Vets are supposed to be called in to prescribe certain drugs to animals. But if there is a risk of bacterial infection, a mass dose of antibiotics will save much trouble.

This abuse of the antimicrobial antibiotic has led to some

peculiar and dangerous immunities. In 1980 and 1981 there were reports in the *British Medical Journal* (*BMJ*) that in the past few years some strains of salmonella were 'multi-resistant' to the commonest antibiotics used in their treatment or prophylaxis; they had been resistant in cattle since 1977, and by 1979 were detected in humans, and were, of course, similarly immune to treatment. One elderly patient and one young child died as result of drug-immune infection, while others had enteritis in various degrees of severity. On 17 May 1980 a *BMJ* paper on the subject finished with an injunction to the veterinary profession:

The responsibility to prevent or control drug resistance in *Salmonella typhimurium* in bovines in Britain lies with the veterinary profession. Such control measures may need the introduction of more stringent regulations governing the use of antibiotics in animals bred for food; clearly the current regulations have failed.

Alan Long condemns milk as a typically dubious product of poisonous husbandry dependent on the profligate use of animal health products. This view is borne out by counts of cells, bacteria and drug residues in British milk and by the dangers that occur if there is a breakdown in the complete pasteurization of milk. In 1981, a report in the *BMJ* spoke of infections by *Campylobacter jejuni*. Between 1978 and early 1981 there had been thirteen documented outbreaks associated with milk (poultry and sheep as well as cattle appear to be sources of the infection). The symptoms are diarrhoea and prostration, and the infection seems to be present in between 5 and 8 per cent of human cases of diarrhoea which are seen by doctors.

Pasteurization kills off *Campylobacter jejuni*, as it kills salmonellas. But 3 per cent of milk in Britain is sold under the Green Top scheme – that is, it is not pasteurized. 70 per cent of such milk is sold in the north of the country. The cases stemmed from various causes, from excessively dirty milk with faecal remnants in one instance, through to breakdowns in the pasteurization system in another. But then, as Alan Long remarks, milk is a food produced in a lavatory: the cow does not know that she must not defecate in the milking parlour. Her infants are immune to many of her diseases, but the general population are not, though farmers' families and farm workers often are.

Salmonella is a small scourge of human populations. It is passed from infected cows into the human food chain whenever pasteurization is eschewed or breaks down. Between 1976 and 1981 milk was established as the source of about 413 reported cases of salmonella poisoning, as against 3,000 cases of campylobacter infection between 1979 and 1981. Poultry meat accounts for many others.

In May 1980, the *BMJ* editorialized on the subject of animals, antibiotics and human infection. The writer noted how the Swann Committee of 1969 had tried to limit the use of antibiotics in animals precisely because there was a danger of drug immunity developing among viral infections common to man and animals. It was decided then to allow regular low dosages of some antibiotics in feed (without a vet's supervision), and to try to preserve some powerful antibiotics as especially effective by limiting their availability to vets and doctors. However, salmonellas were coming into the human food chain through animals, and they were multi-resistant to most antibiotics available to doctors. The *BMJ* commented:

Apart from incautious prescribing, we must look at other factors in seeking to discover why Swann's recommendations [the Swann Committee had suggested ways of preserving the integrity of drugs] have failed in their main objectives – namely, preventing the spread of resistant micro-organisms from farm animals to man.

They outlined as one of the problems the way in which the effectiveness of a drug is undermined by the use of others which are closely enough related to it for bacteria to become immune to both.

Secondly, overenthusiastic representatives of pharmaceutical firms as well as black market operators may find farmers, including poultry producers, all too ready to sidetrack their veterinarians and to bid for any supplies of prescription-only antibiotics that may become available through irregular channels. Thirdly, advertisements in farming papers encourage such attitudes among farmers; this trend needs to be reversed, however delicately and indirectly the hint may be conveyed . . .

The problem of medication in animals is as badly managed as is the problem of medication in people. Quite possibly, the major horror stories of the next century will come from massive immunity by micro-organisms to man's only defence against them, increasingly abused antibiotics. After all, bacteria, no less than any other life-form on earth, are designed by an energetic Providence to be assiduous seekers after life. They have found in our relations with our factory-farmed animals a wide-open highway into the human food chains.

The veterinary profession itself is severely tainted with complicity in the modern factory farmer's depredations upon his animals. It is vets as much as anyone who have designed the systems and developed the techniques which the factory farmer uses. It is vets who dole out the medications which threaten the medicinal basis of many antimicrobials. The entire profession needs to address itself to whether making animals more efficient can seriously, in the light of the severity of modern methods and the calculated overstocking which they involve, be thought of as caring for the animal in their charge as an individual.

On 17 July 1982 a leader in the *Veterinary Record*, the official journal of the British Veterinary Association, drew attention to the problem of misprescribing, but added,

. . . who cannot sympathize with the practice whose important clients lean heavily upon it to supply antibiotics on request 'because if you don't Mr So-and-so will'? Some in consequence may find it difficult to keep their balance on the ethical tightrope relating to the supply of antibiotics to 'animals under his care'.

We can be worried by Jim Morrish's farming, even if his animals – as they do – look patently fit, on the grounds that we suspect that they are probably overdeveloped and are certainly made to endure the yearly calf-theft. However, his way of working will seem positively traditional compared to some of the developments that enthusiastic animal experimenters have developed for the nation's cattle.

Cows have for years been artificially inseminated. But more recently an addition has been made to the technologist farmer's armoury. Cows generally ovulate only one egg at each oestrus, and the national herd average is between three and four calves per cow in a lifetime. However, the ovaries actually contain many thousands of eggs, and the number which are fertilized in premium cows can be increased dramatically by turning the cow into a super-mother. This is achieved by injecting her with hormones (generally Pregnant Mare's Serum Gonadotrophin) which induces super-ovulation.

The embryos are then collected from the super-mother and implanted in lesser cows, whose role is to be used as four-legged incubators and birth machines. Alan Long has dubbed such an unfortunate the 'Blessed Virgin Marigold', or – in the jargon – a maiden heifer. As the Agricultural Research Council's (ARC) *Jubilee Exhibition Brochure* in 1981 explained:

> Non-surgical collection of embryos is performed on the standing cow under local anaesthesia. A rubber or plastic catheter with an inflatable cuff is passed via the vagina into the uterus. The tip of the catheter is directed into the uterine horn and the cuff inflated. The sealed-off uterine horn is flushed with a balanced salt solution. The embryos are located by microscopic examination of the fluid recovered from the uterine flushing ... an average of three to four viable embryos are recovered from each collection, and a cow may serve as a donor five or six times a year.

The embryos are then deep-frozen, using the same techniques as those employed for freezing semen. The scientists have developed means of implanting the embryos in the 'foster' cow by methods close to artificial insemination. However:

> Surgical transfer of embryos via flank incision results in somewhat higher pregnancy rates (65 to 80 per cent versus 45 to 60 per cent) and is therefore still preferred by most commercial groups operating on specially organized premises.

But the day will come, say ARC, when there will not be this need for vivisection.

Jim Morrish was unenthusiastic about too much ultra-modern veterinarian intrusion in his cows' reproductive life. His herd of prize Jerseys – proud boast from the herd society: 'Cream off more profits' – includes cows on their eleventh calf, defying the gloomy average. But his is a pedigree herd of a breed which constitutes only 1 per cent of the dairy herd, though Jim Morrish insists that the majority of dairy farmers are as careful as he is.

But where there are farmers with scruples, they are always under pressure from the price advantage offered by those who are less careful. There have been attempts since the sixties to develop zero-grazed dairy farming, in which cows seldom graze, having all their food brought to them. There is no reason to suppose that this will not be the majority practice soon, with big grants going to farmers who wreck their traditional meadows in favour of rye grass, and the onset of hydroponics.

The calf trade

No dairy farmer can escape the charge that his milk production and everybody's milk consumption depends on the male calves being snatched from their mothers to a fate which altogether undoes any sentimentality that people might like to indulge in about dairy farming. A few good female calves are kept on, to be the milkers of another year. But the rest are destined for meat production, and that especially applies to cows like Jim Morrish's, which are very fine dairy animals but not good beefers. A calf dealer will come to Jim's farm and take the offspring off his hands.

Calf dealers routinely drug their young charges, who will be anything from three days old to about a week or so. The stress of the snatch from their mothers and of journeys in the backs of lorries makes them notoriously prone to disaster. 'A calf's worst enemy is another calf' is an old farmer's adage: calves and infections are inseparable. But worse, calves often do not fetch enough money at the first market they go to, in which case they may be shipped from market to market, weakening all the while, until a decent price can be found for them. One Hoechst vaccination advertisement suggested that 200,000 young calves died every year in diseases associated with stress. It says something for the brutality of this procedure that the National Farmers' Union itself is disturbed by it. These are people who appear totally resistant to any other charge about their factory farming methods, and who always stoutly resist attempts at reform. So we can be very sure that it ought to worry us!

There have been suggestions from the British Veterinary Association that a calf ought to be marked at its first appearance in a market and then not allowed to appear before another one for at least a month. This would induce many dealers to sell them straight away, rather than incur the feeding costs involved in keeping them until they could next appear.

Veal: the luxury of suffering

Every year 20,000 British veal calves are confined in pens which do not allow them to turn round, or even to groom themselves properly. The average such pen, or crate, is 24 inches wide, and when the calf is ready for slaughter at around fourteen weeks of age it fills its prison completely. It will see hardly any light in the course of its life. The result is pale meat.

This system appeals to the curious element in gastronomic life which dictates that the greater the suffering an animal must endure, the greater the sense of luxury its eater will feel. It is tempting to suggest that the pleasure which people take in veal or in pâté de foie gras is not merely that there is a sense that such delicacies often come after long and careful work by dedicated peasants, but also that the subjugation of the animal adds a further element of satisfaction.

Certainly, the origin of veal meat does have a crazy atavistic appeal, like hunting. The traditional veal calf was a very young calf which had lived solely on its mother's milk. Cow's milk being deficient in iron, the meat was pale, and this characteristic, along with tenderness, defines three- or four-month-old calf's meat. The system of calf rearing developed as skimmed milk powder became available. The modern veal calf is a by-product of excessive milk production.

However, most of the myths which led to the cruel crate systems are wrong-headed. Calves were confined in pens because it was thought that if they had bedding or could groom themselves too freely their rumens would develop, leading to poorer milk-to-meat conversion and occasional deaths through disease. It was also thought that the calves must be kept very warm. But this view overlooked the physiological fact that calves were designed to suck from their mothers and that suckling can be simulated in a much freer system of straw-bedded loose housing for groups of around forty calves, using mechanical nipples. When a calf is sucking, the milk it consumes bypasses the rumen altogether, and so it does not matter if it consumes some straw and develops its rumen. Moreover, denying the calf easy access to straw means merely that, despite the difficulty of doing so in its crate, it will find ways of nibbling at its own hair, with the consequent risk of hair balls forming in its stomach.

Thus, after thirty years of shocking and miserable abuse by farmers and consumers, some veal calves are now being allowed a way of life in which they are at least allowed to associate freely with one another (which poses some fresh problems of disease control), even if their one great need – their mothers – is denied them. And that calves want their mothers is best seen by their very touching and practically universal desire to suck at anything – especially a human visitor's thumb and fingers.

But while 40 per cent of the British veal calf stock is now loose-housed, the majority are not. Moreover, there is a pernicious trade of baby calves abroad, especially to Holland, where their fate is the fully intensive system. Compassion in World Farming puts the British importation of crated veal at 90,000 carcases a year. From the consumer's point of view, it is roughly the case that veal bought in the butcher's shop is 90 per cent likely to have been produced in loose-housing, but that almost all the restaurant veal will have been produced by the miserable crate method.

The slaughtering process which a calf goes through is much the same as is supposed to apply for all farm animals. Its preliminaries generally are a distasteful and disagreeable business which many species seem to accept without fuss. Sheep, for instance, can watch their fellows being slaughtered and skinned without a qualm. Pigs, on the other hand, are tremendously prone to anxiety, as anyone can testify who has been around when the slaughterhouse lorry comes to pick them up.

Animals are normally supposed to be rendered unconscious before they are bled out. Various means are employed, including captive bolt guns, electrocuting prods ('stinging') and gassing. There is a good deal of doubt as to whether they are carefully applied in practice, and even whether they always work, however well applied. When they do go wrong, they probably cause more pain than the throat-slitting itself. The captive bolt gun can simply act like a severe blow on the head, for instance.

By long practice both the Jewish and Muslim communities have been allowed to slaughter meat in a way forbidden to the rest of the community. This is so that they may fulfil the requirements of religious laws propounded to preserve the health of carnivorous peoples two thousand years ago. Whatever the rationale, it means that some slaughterhouses some of the time, and a few of them all of the time, kill their animals without prior stunning.

The *Veterinary Record* discussed the problem in an article entitled 'Aspects of Shechita' on 26 September 1981:

> Slaughtering animals is not a pleasant occupation and it is likely that some slaughtermen might lose their correct measure of concern for animal welfare. It is difficult to convince such a person that care must be taken to apply stunning tongs properly when the previous day 100 ewes were (legally) killed without any pre-stunning because they were destined for a specialist market. Concern for animals cannot be varied depending on who is ultimately intended to eat that meat.

There is no doubt, as the author of the article said, that 'the slaughter of animals for food is clearly not an entirely charitable act' and it is likely to be roughly done quite often. It is a case rather like that of farm stockmanship or laboratory experimentation: done well by caring people, pain and misery can be minimized; done badly, untold horrors will be routine.

The Farm Animal Welfare Executive Committee, a group of welfare bodies, has pointed out that the use of electrocution tongs to stun animals requires seven to ten seconds of application to work. Who, after years of life in a slaughter-house and on piecework, will be careful that the full time be accorded the animal, especially since it is also the case that the animal will appear quiet and still long before it is also unconscious?

Argument rages as to the physiological implications of the Jewish method of slaughter, which requires a very rapid cut from a spectacularly sharp and smooth blade on the animal's throat, which is itself presented to the specially trained slaugh-termen extended and with the animal upside down. The cut does not slice the vertebral arteries, and thus there is an active, though reduced, supply of blood to the brain. According to the *Veterinary Record*, 'The animal suffers reflex convulsions some five to ten seconds later, although whether it actually suffers pain as well remains a topic for argument.' The journal also noted that it is claimed that the last moments before slaughter induce a state like shock in the animals, and that this amounts to a substitute for pre-slaughter stunning. Some Muslim opinion is less demanding than most Jewish, and many Muslim religious authorities accept pre-slaughter stunning. According to Alan Long in the *Vegetarian*, the Muslim ritual includes the utterances (it may be silent) of a prayer begging forgiveness of Allah for taking one of His creatures.

Long has attended Shechita slaughter, and wrote of the bedlam that took place in the building:

The term 'religious slaughter' seemed unapt for such debauchery. The design of the casting pen [which capsizes and restrains the animals] was atrocious. The beasts had to negotiate a decline into the pen, they faced all the scenes of slaughter and butchery in the hall, and they heard the din of the machinery. They were driven apprehensive into the pen, bolts were driven home, and a man rotated it. The animal's bellowing began as the cage clanked shut. Terrified at being overturned, it began its furious struggles to escape. A half-ton bullock wriggling like a puppy might wrench a limb free. Thrashing about, it would dash its head repeatedly on the concrete floor . . . After nearly a minute of this agony the animal surrendered to the cut.

Because of Jewish fastidiousness about the quality of their meat, nearly a third of the animals slaughtered for their

onsumption is not passed by them; instead, it reaches the
rdinary market, undistinguished from normally slaughtered
neat. Moreover, the Jewish community does not eat all of the
nimal, and therefore over half the animal meat slaughtered
ccording to Jewish custom is eaten by people who might
ery well be strongly opposed to animals being slaughtered
while sentient.

Alan Long knows perfectly well that people who criticize
ewish or Muslim practices may be open to the charge of fuel-
ng prejudice against those minorities. However, he counters
nis by saying:

> As vegetarians, we can appeal sincerely to Jews and Muslims. As one
> minority to another, we can beseech them to do as we do, with no
> infringement of their beliefs or culture; indeed, by abandoning such
> alien practices they would surely ennoble their influence on the com-
> munity. The vigour of the Jewish Vegetarian Society attests to a
> willingness to forgo the products of torture. Muslims expect their vis-
> itors to respect their teachings over alcohol and they punish transgres-
> sors. We may sincerely ask them to desist here from practices offensive
> to the traditions of the British population.

In the meantime, there is a thriving slaughterhouse business
providing ritually slaughtered meat for the Muslim trade both
n Britain and abroad. It seems to insist on ignoring the definite
nd well-documented Muslim authorities who have eschewed
ne slaughtering of animals while sentient.

The slaughtering, marketing and transport of animals for
neat have become major issues in animal welfare in recent
ears. There is increasing concern that the trade in live animals
or export ought to be far more strictly regulated. Long tradition
as led to entrenched abuses. In all of them, people are
rendered careless and indifferent by the dreary, humdrum and
undamental cruelty of their work. Economics and dietary
abits combine with a distaste for the unpleasant to make a
publicity campaign hard to mount. The public is embarrassed
y its own indifference to miserable trades.

Working for reforms

Consumers expect cheap food, and in general have so far bee
wholly indifferent to animal misery. This may be because the
are ignorant of the suffering. It may be because the pangs
conscience are indulged in only for the duration of a televisic
programme on the subject, but do not wield much authori
when the customer is leaning over the fridge in the supe
market.

The cheap food mentality has led to a lack of appreciation
celebration of the things which give us sustenance. The huma
contract with the life around us, from which we gain our life
blood, has been broken. In some quite important sense, we ca
have factory farms, in which animals never see any kind
natural life and have no identity with those who husband then
because we consumers have lost our interest in what gives u
sustenance. We want it to pass health checks; we want to com
to no harm from what we eat; we are not interested in how
came to us, provided that it comes at a reasonable price.

On the other hand, we are near – many people believe – to
kind of breakthrough point. Animals are acquiring a new ro
and status in people's consciousness. With luck, the fascinatio
that wildlife holds for people today may one day extend to th
creatures we first domesticated and then put into factorie
People may be ready to see the ironies here: the animals whic
were once 'domesticated' (i.e. rendered homely) have becom
victims of industrialization. Most people have only to b
properly aware of that peculiarity to be revolted by it.

The welfare organizations have been arguing that the
ought to be a label on veal at least, detailing the means
production. They are backed in this by the Volac compan
which produces a high proportion of the British loose-house
calves. But since Britain's entry into the EEC, governments a
always able to say, and usually do, that any restriction on cru
food production would merely put us at a disadvantage vis-
vis our less conscience-stricken fellow members. Britain, und
EEC regulation, is forbidden to impose any sort of unilater
controls on foreign products. This means that the governme

des behind EEC regulations in defending brutal agriculture, cked strongly by the National Farmers' Union, which always rongly resists any attempt to reform farming (and which itself smissed most of the Agriculture Committee's rather humane dings and appears to have prevailed upon agriculture nisters to take the same line).

We cannot look to governments to protect our consciences. e cannot look to many farmers to eschew profit or their decent ings in favour of humane production. More humane production will come about only if consumers refuse to sustain themlves and their families on the products of cruelty.

The representatives of the consumer at the Agriculture ommittee's hearing went out of their way to stress that price, d not humanity, is what characterizes the consumer's iorities at the till. Mrs Graham, a member of the executive mmittee of the National Federation of Consumer Groups and ember of the Eggs Authority, echoed the other members of omen's Institutes and Consumer Councils in saying about the usewife's concern for humane production:

I think it might affect them for a short time; but when they look ound and they see what they can buy with the money in their purses d they realize that eggs, and perhaps chickens, provide the cheapest rm of protein, I am afraid we are back to economy. I think they would el sorry for the chickens and the hens, but I think their stomachs uld win in the end.

rs Clark-Glass, a member of the National Consumer Council, as yet more blunt:

There have been very effective programmes on television, and those ave not made an appreciable difference to the buying patterns of nsumers. Consumers are far more concerned by how much they have their purses or pocket, I am afraid, than animal welfare.

It needs to be said here that the obsession with protein and eapness of protein is wholly unnecessary. In 1972 it was und that in no income bracket of the nation was there anying like protein deficiency as described by high Western stanards, which are themselves well above the minimum require-ents. Taking the sort of family which might be expected to

be doing poorly in their diet, with two adults and four or mo
children, even the poorest households were consuming 11 p
cent more protein than the recommended intake, and better-c
households consumed around 14 per cent more.

Leaving aside the debate about people's requirement f
dietary intake of animal products, it is clear that there is no nee
for the British consumer to feel hard done by: at the *very leas*
almost all households could cut back on meat consumption 1
10 per cent with no adverse consequences to their prote
intake. Expressed another way, housewives could easily allo
a humane production system to produce 10 per cent less me
for its current cost, and could buy 10 per cent less, but human
meat for their weekly budget, before they need even begin
ask themselves if their protein intake was anything less th
very generous. The *British Medical Journal* has already called f
a 15 per cent reduction in meat consumption as part of a 'Pr
scription for a Better British Diet'.

Against the pressures of economics and technologic
advance, the welfarists do their best to refine and tighten t
codes which are supposed to regulate the treatment of farme
animals. The Commons Agriculture Committee made its poli
recommendations for increased space and fewer surgic
depredations for various animals. The Farm Animal Welfa
Council advises and promotes broadly similar notions. But,
usual, change is painfully slow. The European Commission
studying some aspects of farm animal welfare. Every dra
proposal for a directive binding on all EEC members provides
rich ground for long-winded discussions behind whi
ministers can safely shelter while listening attentively
counter-representations made to them by the Nation
Farmers' Union, which always stresses the primacy of the co
sumer and even pretends that intensive farming is good f
animals.

Such as it is, the Ministry of Agriculture, Fisheries and Food
inspection of factory farms is done by people who may regr
but see no chance of seriously reforming modern agricultur
methods. The codes are recommendations only (though igno
ing them is supposed to go towards establishing a prima-fac

case of cruelty). They are ignored with impunity by almost all factory farmers, who – with the connivance of the MAFF – simply insist that they know better. In exactly the same way as the Home Office inspectorate deals with laboratory animals, the inspectors are determined that they must be the 'farmer's friend' or else their policing job will not merely be inherently impossible, it will be thwarted actively at every turn by their farmer clients. The inspectors are in any case also the people who advise farmers on how to make animals more productive, with the health of individual animals necessarily taking second place.

3

ANIMALS IN LABORATORIES

The laboratory animal has all the iniquities that man has designed for animals heaped upon it. It is bred, stolen or captured. It is kept in captivity, and usually in an environment which makes no concessions whatever to its ethological needs. It is 'used' (a word which seems odd in the context, as though an animal were a car or a food-mixer) with a greater or lesser degree of pain for purposes to which it cannot give assent.

If the animal survives its first encounter with the experimenter, then very probably it will merely be saved for another. Unless to be an animal in pain is so different from being a person in pain that there would be very little point in using it as a model for the conditions to which we are prone, to be a laboratory animal is to be a professional recipient of pain or distress whose only relief is a premature death.

The 1876 Cruelty to Animals Act, the animal's sole defender (except for the consciences of scientists and the activities of the Animal Liberation Front), according to the Home Office's interpretation, regulates an experiment only if 'it is considered . . . it presents a risk of pain, distress, discomfort or interference with an animal's ordinary state of health or well-being'. A total of 4·34 million experiments were reported in 1981, though this represents 250,000 fewer than in 1980 and the lowest number since 1963.

The Act's own terms tell us that every experiment involves an animal either suffering – and sometimes suffering a very great deal as a crucial and deliberate part of the experiment – or at the very least being made either unhappy or ill. And we have to remember that fact when we look at the cool statistics which

he Home Office publishes every year (in greater detail than
ised to be the case). Here is a selection culled from the 1981
igures.

1. Over 1·69 million experiments were conducted for 'the selection of potential medical, dental or veterinary products and
   appliances', but with no mention of whether the potential
   was fulfilled, or whether the products already existed on the
   market under another name or made by another laboratory.

2. Nearly 19,000 endured 'application of substance to the eye'
   (down a third since 1977).

3. 92,300 endured 'interference with the central nervous
   system' (down from 150,000 in 1977).

4. 24,000 experiments were conducted 'to select, develop or
   study the use, hazards or safety of cosmetics and toiletries'
   (down to its 1977 level after peaking in 1980).

5. At the very least, 824,000 experiments are conducted to fulfil
   the requirements imposed by British or overseas legislation
   (some of which require several experiments for each substance because there is not necessarily conformity of test
   requirement between countries).

6. 15 members of the Home Office inspectorate are supposed to
   be able to monitor and control 527 registered laboratories
   wherein 12,000 active licence-holders do their work.

7. 4,800 animals, half of them rats, endured 'infliction of physical trauma to simulate human injury, other than by burning
   or scalding', which 2,787 animals suffered. Both these types
   of experiment are increasing in number: the former was up
   nearly two thirds, the latter up by almost a third.

But these official statistics are impossible to analyse or inter-
pret. Some of the categories lump together research work,
which it would be quite easy to argue is serious, with routine
trawling by drug companies for look-alike drugs which may
well be made by a competitor but which a firm likes to be able to
imitate and have in its own stable. The discovery and then the
safety testing of such a substance would involve animal

research. The figures lump together work which is done to test the safety-in-use of products whose use is valuable with test on wholly trivial things.

Extraordinary stories filter through to the press. The Scottish Society for the Prevention of Vivisection (SSPV) *Annual Pictorial Review 1982* quoted this report of work done at Stirling University and published in the American Journal, *Visual Impairment and Blindness*:

Eight stump-tailed Macaques [monkeys] were separated from their mothers within one week of birth. They were reared alone in cage where they could not see other infant monkeys, although they could hear and smell them.

After three months in solitary confinement the monkeys were allowed to meet each other, but four of them did so in total darkness. The object was to assess the behaviour of the 'blind monkeys', which it was claimed could provide vital information on the behaviour of blind children. The project was funded by the Science Research Council out of tax-payers' money. The researchers noted that the 'blind' monkeys were almost totally lacking in aggression. They used no threats or bites. The headmaster of the Royal Blind School in Edinburgh said that he was not interested in the work: 'The behaviour of blind children is more likely to be affected by their personal relations, the expectations of their parents and their involvement with other people. Some were aggressive because of the frustrations and pressures of blindness, while other remained completely placid.'

The scientists involved in this work would have to be very persuasive to get across to ordinary people – say a jury – that the work could tell science much, and that it might tell scientists more what happens to Macaque babies who are denied all social life, rather than to blind Macaques or blind human babies. Nonetheless, as the SSPV continued:

In answer to a parliamentary question on these experiments, Baroness Young confirmed the Home Secretary's authorization, details of the work done and the funding, and stated: 'This grant was for fundamental research in the field of early primate development and the respective importance of different factors influencing behaviour. Results from earlier research of this type had contributed significantly to the understanding and care of developing children.'

he scientific community and the government (and charities) which fund them are bound to close ranks: the first have their careers to think of, and the second do not like it thought that they have wasted or abused tax-payers' money.

Experiments in which severe pain is caused are not common, but the enormous number of animals on which are inflicted the miseries of cages, absence of family or social life, and constant low levels of pain or discomfort is just as serious.

Nonetheless, there are cases where research journals report very controversial work. For instance, *The Journal of Pharmacological Methods* in 1978 published 'A Method for Evaluating Potential Hypnotic Compounds in Rats', written by workers at Roussell, a major commercial drug house, who had created 'an animal model of consistent "insomnia" for testing candidate hypnotic agents'. This amounted to giving large numbers of rats electric shocks on the feet in order to test the possibility of marketing yet another sleeping pill.

The 1876 Act

What sort of law is it that can allow such nonsenses as have been described in the last section, and under which it is so hard to tempt, cajole or force scientists to give a better account of themselves?

The 1876 Cruelty to Animals Act, which imposes limits upon what experiments may be done, is not a cruel thing in itself, and has been interpreted quite broadly to try to bring it into the twentieth century. However, it is a charter for the scientific community to be judge and jury in its own cause, and to perform distasteful acts in what is a very indecent obscurity. It has serious gaps in the protection which it gives to animals and which the late-nineteenth-century framers of the Act did not think of, mostly because they involve procedures which had not been thought of when the Act came into force. These include the use of animals to grow tumours for research into cancer, and the use of animals to produce some types of vaccines. The Act describes a procedure as an experiment only if a question is being asked, but in tumour growth and vaccine

production the conclusion is known, and hence there is n
coverage by the Act. But no other Act seriously polices suc
usages either.

The scale of the problem is difficult to assess. There are n
statistics available, though the Association of the British Phar
maceutical Industry told the House of Lords Select Committe
on the Laboratory Animals Protection Bill that they though
50,000 animals were used in the production of anti-sera alone.

One of the most famous abuses of animals, revealed in earl
1975 by the *Sunday People* (tipped off by animal welfarists), wa
the 'smoking beagles' research done by ICI, in which beagl
dogs had been made to smoke cigarettes. It would not hav
occurred to the Victorian legislator to wonder whether or ne
beagles should be subjected to involuntary smoking, an
perhaps it would not have occurred to him that the public, onc
alerted to the use of dogs in smoking tests, would allow othe
animals to undergo them, provided only they were not beagle
(though, apparently, most of the animals now used to fin
ways of providing relief for recalcitrant smokers do not actuall
have to smoke cigarettes – they are made to 'slipstream' smok
instead).

A London teaching hospital has been force-feeding monkey
with confectionery to see if a better way of fighting tooth deca
can be found. Neither smoking nor eating confectionery ar
things which animals do in what is left of the wild, or thing
which people need to do in the midst of civilization. But no on
has yet found a way of describing the misery of cancer or othe
smoking-induced diseases, or even of visits to the dentist, a
other than serious, and therefore smoking and sweet-eatin
become subjects meriting animal research.

The Victorians did not undergo the kind of anxiety abou
public safety which we feel today, and therefore did not engag
in the often less-than-accurate experiments which attempt t
assuage it by employing animals in such as the irritancy te
invented in 1944 by Draize, in which the eyes of live anima
(usually rabbits) are used as a yardstick of sensitivity in testin
for damaging effects. The Draize test has been severely crit
cized on practical grounds of validity, as well as being s

obviously unpleasant that welfarists have found it a useful lever on public opinion. There have been some attempts to improve on it by using the well-preserved eyeballs of dead rabbits.

Another modern invention which the Victorians might have blanched at is the LD50 test. It sounds like something in the mould of 'overkill', and indeed it works very like the nuclear war concept known as 'Circular Error Probable' (CEP – by which one can estimate the accuracy of a weapon system – is the radius of a circle of which the centre is the target, and within which 50 per cent of missiles targeted on the centre are likely to fall). LD50 tests were devised in 1929. Properly called 'Lethal Dose 50 per cent', it is a statistical estimate of the dose of a substance which would kill half the animals of a group. It involves finding the dose which will kill animals, and the more animals used, the more accurate it is. However, it does not tell us anything about the long-term effects of exposure to toxic substances. It has been criticized not least because it is possible to establish as much as one usually needs by accurate observation of the dose which affects animals rather than kills them. But more of the LD50 later; enough now to say that perhaps a quarter of a million LD50's are done every year (that was the best bet in 1977), and that now they are mostly used in testing the safety of new substances rather than the purity and safety of well-known ones.

The 1876 Act was designed to work within a framework in which science and scientists were in general assumed to be trustworthy in their objects and in the reasons for which they might use animals. Since then, we have become more sceptical and scientists have become more profligate. Yet the most important means of policing the Act remain appropriate only to the problems that its framers found over a hundred years ago. In 1885 there were 53 licensees working in 13 registered laboratories; today there are over 20,000 licensees (of whom more than half are active) working in 527 registered places, and about 10,000 times as many experiments are now done annually compared to a hundred years ago. It is clear that science has added new procedures, new purposes (or lack of them) and new numbers to the animal experimenters and their animals, as well as a new scepticism about what they do. Yet it is professional researchers or scientific academics (strictly speaking, the Act specifies the president of a learned society and a professor of a branch of medical science) who alone must countersign as sponsors a candidate's application to experiment under the Act.

The Act, as it has come to be interpreted, gives protection to *vertebrate animals only*, by making it a requirement that any experiment which *'presents a risk of pain, distress, discomfort or interference with the animal's ordinary state of health or well-being'* may only be made by a licensed person in a registered laboratory. Quoting the *Statistics of Experiments on Living Animals*:

> The Act prohibits absolutely any experiment performed for the purpose of attaining manual skill or for purposes other than the advancement by new discovery of physiological knowledge or of knowledge which will be useful in saving or prolonging life or alleviating suffering, or the acquisition of such knowledge by persons attending lectures in medical schools, hospitals or elsewhere.

 In principle, animals are not supposed to be hurt or made miserable:

> Where an animal is likely to suffer under the experiment it must be anaesthetized, and if it is likely to suffer when it comes round, be killed before it is allowed to do so.

However, the strictness and protectiveness of many of these rules are mitigated in the experimenters' favour by various certificates which can be, and in over 80 per cent of experiments are, obtained by experimenters, and most of which have the effect of weakening the Act. The vast majority of experiments are conducted under Certificate A, which allows experiments to be conducted without anaesthetics, and under Certificate B, which allows an animal to recover from an anaesthetic, even if it will be in pain when it comes round. Other certificates must be obtained if an experimenter believes he needs to use cats, dogs, horses, asses or mules, or to perform an experiment for the illustration of a lecture.

Beyond that there are conditions (the second of the tiers of conventions and rules which have accreted around the Act) which insist that, even under Certificate A, only fairly simple operative procedures should be carried out on an animal (which does not help the animal much, says Richard Ryder, a former RSPCA chairman and a noted animal welfare campaigner, since most of the painful procedures to be carried out under Certificate A are not operative procedures anyway).

A further condition is attached to all Certificates A and B. Again quoting from the *Statistics of Experiments on Living Animals*:

> If any animal at any time during any of the said experiments under the said certificate is found to be suffering pain which is either severe or is likely to endure, and if the main result of the experiment has been attained, the animal shall forthwith be painlessly killed.
>
> If any animal at any time during any of the said experiments is found to be suffering severe pain which is likely to endure, such animal shall forthwith be painlessly killed.
>
> If any animal appears to an inspector to be suffering considerable pain, and if such inspector directs such animal to be destroyed, it shall forthwith be painlessly killed.

One has to study hard these paragraphs of what is known as the 'Pain Condition'. The distinction then becomes clear: animals must, under these conditions, be expected to bear *either* severe pain *or* pain which is likely to endure; but they are excused continued suffering of pain which is *both* severe and enduring, once, that is, they have been found to be suffering pain which is likely to be so.

There is unlimited scope for abuse here. It may be rare or uncharacteristic abuse, and it may be abuse which is deeply shocking to the majority of scientists; but the terms of the condition clearly give scope for abuse by a scientist temporarily or peculiarly over-keen, for instance, to see the results of his work come right, and inclined, for the relevant minutes or hours, to give himself and not the animal the benefit of the doubt as to whether he, the scientist, has yet spotted the animal's suffering pain which is (a) severe *and* (b) likely to be prolonged. And, certainly, the campaigners against the Act, or rather for its reform, come back to this theme again and again.

But they have plenty of other complaints to make, and increasingly their arguments are gaining strength and support.

Modern scientists and their animals

Scientists are brought up within a particular framework which is inclined to overestimate the value of finding the answer to any question that human curiosity proposes, and which, through constant familiarity, is inclined to underestimate the potential for the misery of animals.

It begins in school, where the burgeoning movement for humane education is establishing a grip in children's minds akin to the role of CND. Until recently, biology students carved up small animals with hardly a thought. According to a *Times Educational Supplement* report headlined 'Pupils' anti-dissection rebellion grows', published on 16 July 1982, some pupils are already insisting – with markedly varying response from their teachers – on tackling A-level Biology without sullying their hands or consciences with dissecting practice of any kind. It is nevertheless true that some scientists are becoming very concerned about researchers' attitudes to animal research. According to a Royal Society and Institute of Biology survey carried out in the mid-seventies, around 250,000 animals were cut up annually by children in schools (the tally included 130,000 rats, 50,000 dogfish and 45,000 frogs, while rabbits, earthworms, mice, guinea pigs and 'innumerable' insects were also used).

A BBC *Panorama* film on test-tube babies (2 August 1982) showed scientists working on living embryos from monkeys; but another senior scientist said that such work is irrelevant for human comparison, and that he was worried that there were greater, not lesser, problems to be had in using animal embryos for doing work which had only human application. The implication was that he thought that we ought to face the full moral dilemma, and use only human embryos for such work (which leaves aside, of course, the question of whether the work is in any case justifiable).

Science has become very profligate indeed. It can dream up

new questions and new approaches to answering them terribly
easily. Graduates come tumbling out of universities with clever
projects to obtain tax-payers' money from the research-funding
bodies. And scientists have devised a very powerful establishment to protect their right to be curious which matches the
manufacturers' cry of satisfying consumer choice.

When Lord Houghton, during the House of Lords inquiry,
raised some of the awkward questions, he was told by the
witness from the Association for the Study of Animal Behaviour
that

it is part of the evidence my Association has given that experiments
should be licensed, and that they should be subject to proper control. It
is very easy to play the game of saying that this, that or the other
experiments in any field of science are trivial. However, what an outsider must never forget is that scientists are engaged in the business of
building an edifice of knowledge, and sometimes even relatively trivial
or seemingly trivial experiments, trivial bits of knowledge, have to be
specified in a precise way, so that they can properly be added to that
edifice of knowledge. It is very difficult for the outsider to judge what is
trivial and what is not. In my view this is the proper province of the
licensing authorities and of the people who sign applications for
licences.

This is the ancient cry of privilege and expertise, which citizens
everywhere are learning to suspect. It is the kind of answer
which makes progress in a discussion impossible. It simply
asserts that no scientist, and certainly no layman, can tell what
unexpected benefits will accrue from a piece of research; it
shelters behind the possibility that every cloud may have a
silver lining; and it particularly leads into another favourite
argument of the researchers – namely, that what they are doing
is an experiment, so of course they do not know what the
benefit will be. To know what the benefit will be, they would
have at the very least to know what the result will be, in which
case, they are able to say, the thing would not be an experiment
at all.

Richard Ryder's essay in *Animals in Research* cites the late
Professor Smyth (one-time chairman of the Research Defence
Society) as saying that he thought that not one in 3,000

substances experimented on in laboratories produced anything valuable. Lord Perry (one-time chairman of the Research
Defence Society) once told me that 99 per cent of research
turned out to be useless (however, he later suggested that the
figure was probably not that high, but he explains that the
apparent waste is an inevitable price of progress in research).
Clearly research is, like many human activities, more of a hit-
and-miss affair than would be tidy and agreeable. But if the
benefits still accrue, then who is to say that the research should
not be undertaken?

This logic has generated a massive and growing habit in the
research industries to 'trawl' for answers to problems. A drug
company or a 'pure' researcher alike find themselves pursuing
problems with an unassailable rationale behind them. We do
not know enough about the world's natural phenomena to be
more than thoroughly exploratory in our techniques. How sight
is developed in children, or what are the properties of a newly
synthesized substance, are both, in various degrees,
unknowns, and at least allow the scientists to proceed to subject
animals to experiments. The animals' sight can be used as a
model for human sight, and the animals' reactions can be used
as a model for the substance's effect on a human physiology.
The scientist is able to say that he asked himself a serious
question which it would be incurious at the very least not to try
to answer. And the drug researcher is able to say that the
substance he is working on may be the one which cures some
major medical problem.

Some of the results seem plain and excellent enough. Dr
David Owen, now of the Social Democratic Party, was reported
in the *Sunday Times* of 30 October 1976 as saying:

A hundred years ago a boy at birth could expect to live forty-one years
and a girl forty-five. Only six babies out of ten survived until adulthood.
Since the last century improved health measures, housing, nutrition
and other factors have reduced deaths from tuberculosis, typhoid,
diphtheria, scarlet fever, whooping cough and measles by ninety per
cent.

These are all advances that are put down to classical medical
research, all involving animal research in the initial discovery or

in the production of sera or in batch testing for safety of vaccines and drugs.

But the story is far more complicated than science fans might imagine. A sober and considered booklet produced by the British Office of Health Economics, written by its director, Professor George Teeling-Smith, is concerned not to overestimate the degree to which medical science can claim the credit for the advances. In *A Question of Balance: The Benefits and Risks of Pharmaceutical Innovation*, the author states:

Of course, much of the reduction in mortality in the past century has been part of a long-term trend in the improvement in health due to better nutrition, better housing and sanitation, and reduction in poverty and squalor generally. However, those who argue that modern medical progress has contributed little or nothing by comparison seriously overstate their case ... There have been very many specific and dramatic improvements in health status due to modern pharmaceutical progress. The first and universally accepted example is with tuberculosis. Mortality from this cause had already been declining during the latter part of the nineteenth century to an annual rate of about 150 deaths per 100,000 by 1900. After that, with the exception of the two world wars, mortality continued to decline until the mid 1940s, when it accounted for 50 deaths per 100,000. However, there were still long waiting-lists for the crowded tuberculosis sanitaria, with over 30,000 beds occupied by tuberculosis patients. At that point, with the introduction of streptomycin, isoniazid and para-aminobenzoic acid, there was a sharp decline in mortality. By 1976 the death rate had fallen to about 2 per 100,000.

Professor Teeling-Smith mentions some of the other cases: vaccines for diphtheria, measles and whooping cough; antibiotics for pneumonia and meningitis. Most of these advances have controversies surrounding them, including reactions from vaccines, and immunity by some bacteria to antibiotics. They all have their difficulties, and are wide open for serious discussion on ethical grounds. But Professor Teeling-Smith says that a quarter of a million people are alive today who would have died from childhood diseases without such advances.

We can surely agree that we do not know how to dismiss such a statistic as trumped-up or a matter of indifference. And no one seemed to know how to get such advances without animal research. But we should remember that in other areas of medicine the kind of technological progress which we have made is very seriously open to doubt. As David Owen wrote:

A man aged fifty in 1841, when reliable records began, could expect to live a further twenty years; by 1972–4 a man aged fifty could expect to live another twenty-three years. So, despite the improvements in health care in the intervening time, life expectancy had increased by just three years.

The anti-vivisectionists are fond of quoting the thalidomide tragedy of the early sixties as a classic case of a drug which passed its animal tests and was still highly dangerous. A drug developed as a tranquillizer turned out to be teratogenic (i.e. it affected the growth of the foetus): used by pregnant mothers, it could produce deformed babies. In 1962, even after it was withdrawn, between 400 and 500 babies were born with defects because the effects originated in the first three months of pregnancy and had been set in train by the time that it was suspected.

The British government immediately found itself pressured into taking a much stricter role in the licensing of drugs. Committees proliferated. Tests for safety were tightened up. Drugs had now to be tested for teratogenicity, and multi-species animal testing was introduced. Along with the rising tide of consumerism, in which people must be made safe from the ill effects of doing all sorts of things and using all sorts of products, there were increasing legislative and quasi-legislative gentlemen's agreements which added massively to the expense of medical advance, both in money and in animals. One of the effects of the increased desire for stringency was to slow down much pharmaceutical activity. There are drugs with pretty well-known benefits and probable small risk which cannot be introduced to the ordinary drug market because their potential market is small and they cannot pay their way through the new regulatory hoops (though in some cases they can be made by hospital laboratories without the same inhibitions).

But there are important things to be said about the new

demands for safety. Teeling-Smith quotes Enoch Powell, the Minister for Health from 1960 to 1963:

It would be a cruel deception, to which no man of science or professional integrity would lend himself, to pretend that this or any other mechanism can guarantee absolute safety or indeed that, in this field, such a thing as absolute safety exists at all. Our knowledge is imperfect, and as long as pharmaceutical science advances, it will necessarily continue to be imperfect though constantly widening ... There is at present no hard evidence to show the value of more extensive and more prolonged laboratory testing as a method of reducing eventual risk in human patients. In other words, the predictive value of studies carried out in animals is uncertain. The statutory bodies such as the Committee on the Safety of Medicines which require these tests do so largely as an act of faith rather than on hard scientific grounds.

It is as though we had to trust insurance companies who would offer us protection, but only sometimes – say, for instance, provided the injury we suffered occurred in months with an 'r' in them. It is not good insurance, but it is the best on offer. The passage continues:

With thalidomide, for example, it is only possible to produce the specific deformities in a very small number of species. In this particular case, therefore, it is unlikely that specific tests in pregnant animals would have given the necessary warning: the right species would probably never have been used.

In some cases of very dangerous side-effects it has been found impossible to find a species which reacted to the substance in the same (awful) way that humans did. And the thought continues:

Conversely, penicillin in very small doses is fatal to guinea pigs. If it had been tested in those animals before being given to man, its systemic use in humans might well have been considered to be hazardous and unethical. Hence the first problem in minimizing risks with new medicines is the difficulty inherent in trying to predict adverse reactions in man from studies in experimental animals. The present tendency is to ask for more and longer animal tests merely in the hope that they may somehow make medicines safer.

The author suggests that though there were changes in testing procedures as a result of the thalidomide tragedy, there is 'no evidence from the United States experience with thalidomide that more prolonged laboratory testing as such would have avoided the human tragedy'.

Animal research does not make science risk-free. And it is not always seriously designed to get an answer. Discussing a kind of excess in testing which can happen, Teeling-Smith cites the American requirement that no substance which is shown to be capable of producing cancer in an animal can be marketed. The British, he says, have followed the same kind of pattern of practice:

One of the most recent examples has been the withdrawal of the antihistamine methapyrilene from the British market on the advice of the Committee on Safety of Medicines. The compound had been shown to be able to produce tumours in rats when administered continuously through their lives at 25 to 30 times the dose appropriate to man.

No one thought that such a ban was other than a 'precautionary arrangement'. No one would claim that such a ban was based on tight evidence. There is not much more here than the casting of entrails.

There has been a good deal of discussion about the proliferation of look-alike drugs which do not individually provide a particularly useful new cure for an ailment, but which provide the manufacturer with a marketable and patentable new entity. In the *British Journal of Clinical Pharmacology* (1981, 12, pp. 453–63) two Department of Health and Social Security officials, J. B. Griffin and G. E. Diggle, published a damning review, based on the Department's experience of licensing medicines. Taking the idea of the New Chemical Entity (NCE), which implies substances which are new to science or newly made and which stand a chance, therefore, of advancing therapeutic medicine, they found that the Department was licensing more and more variations on old themes and a constant or declining number of NCEs. In the decade up to 1980, the number of licences for substances which were only variations rose from 1,800 to 6,898, while the number of NCEs was 37 in 1971 and 23 in 1981.

They say, and regret, that commercial pressure has proved

stronger than concern for scientific originality and often over-
rides

therapeutic principles, with the result that an abundance of analogous
drugs are offered, not rarely with exaggerated claims for efficacy. We
now witness the Beta-adenrenoceptor blockers and many remember a
comparable situation for the antihistamines about twenty-five years
ago, when the drug regulations were very much less strict than they are
today. We have a plethora of closely related penicillin and cephalospo-
rin derivatives, of topical corticosteroids, of diuretics, or of minor tran-
quillizers. Here a self-restriction of the pharmaceutical companies
would be most useful and recommendable and might contribute to the
credibility of the arguments issued by the drug industry. However, the
temptation to look for a share of a big cake exceeds only too often
rational and scientific thinking. It should always be kept in mind that
the main impulse for the development of a new drug is the therapeutic
need, and that, if a disease can already be effectively treated, a new
medicine must offer advantages which are more than marginal.

These are not, remember, the arguments of an animal welfare
paper, issued by commerce-bashing radicals: they are from two
authorities working for the government watchdog of drug efficacy and safety. They are supervising an industry in which
3,000 drug salesmen peddle medicines to British doctors, who
write out 345 million prescriptions a year.

We have been warned to consider the value of much drug
company research. But how much effort ought we to put into
making it safe for people to do trivial things? Is a manufacturer
or a safety authority remiss if they have not found out how
many pints or gallons of this or that chemical cleaner will kill a
child if it is perfectly obvious that the child should not have been
allowed to drink down any of the stuff at all? It is of course sad
that little Johnny is ill and must have his stomach pumped, and
everyone hopes that his treatment will be successful. But how
precisely should we know how much would kill him (even if
such a thing were knowable with the precision pretended)? Is it
draconian to say that there are some things it is not worth being
precise about, especially if we know how to solve the problems
which they present?

In *Of Acceptable Risk: Science and the Determination of Safety*,

William Laurance discusses the case of the banning of cycla-
mates in the late sixties. At the time, evidence against them was
that

a 12-ounce bottle of soft drink may have contained from a quarter to a
gram of sodium cyclamate. An adult would have had to drink from 138
to 552 12-ounce bottles of soft drink a day to get an amount causing
cancer in mice and rats.

Anyone who drank that amount of pop would be bound to die
of something!

In a recent paper, two cosmetic company researchers, trying
to establish some sort of sensible criteria for risk acceptability,
quoted reports which variously believed that individuals were
worried about risks when they stood in a probability of from 1 in
7,500 to 1 in 10 million. But Laurance noted the famous statistic
that Americans seemed happy enough with risks from death by
car accident in a range of 1 in 4,000 (since 1 in 4,000 Americans
died in car accidents in 1976 and no one gave up cars on that
account).

Animals suffer to make us safe from our folly and from our
triviality. They suffer so that we can discover new substances,
and many not so new substances. We know also that they suffer
mightily from the 'pure' research of physiologists, psycholog-
ists and others. Animal welfarists have been scanning research
journals to try to understand what sort of work is going on,
whether it is valuable, and whether its use of animals was
directed at what have been identified several times now as the
Three Rs. The Three Rs were so called by Burch and Russell in
The Principles of Humane Experimental Technique. The researcher
applying the Three Rs seeks (a) to Reduce the number of
animals he uses; (b) to Replace the animals by alternative means
of research; and (c) to Refine techniques so that pain and distress to animals can be eliminated or reduced.

The particular value of asking such questions is that it goes a
long way towards answering a problem which scientists like to
hide behind in justifying their work. They say that it is impossible to provide proper ethical scrutiny for all the immensity
of work which is done. However, it would be possible to

scrutinize a selection of the research papers and animal research applications so as to build up a case law as to what seemed worth doing and what had seemed excessive or redundant.

Professor Patrick Wall of University College, London, is editor of the journal *Pain* and chairman of the Grants Committee of the Neurological Science Board of the Medical Research Council. He has been an important 'dove' in the science world on the business of causing pain to animals, and he says:

I am very sorry to say that there are real situations where research on animals is necessary. But we now insist on certain requirements of the authors of papers submitted to *Pain*. We insist that the researcher use the lowest species of animal possible ... We want to know that the author has thought carefully about whether or not his experiment has a reasonable chance of having a practical consequence: curiosity alone – which is usually important in science – isn't regarded as good enough. And we want to know that the minimum number of animals has been used for the shortest amount of time.

Professor Wall would be happy to see ethical scrutiny extended to grant applications (which are very detailed) and to licence applications. He wrote on the subject in an editorial in *Pain*:

We cannot expect governments to generate precise regulations which would both protect animals and allow crucial experiments under all circumstances. As working scientists who care for animals, we may on occasions forbid an experiment even though it fulfils the laws of our country, and on other occasions we may campaign for an experiment which laws have restricted. It seems to me that we should consult widely *before* starting an experiment when these issues are in doubt. As new challenges arise, the problems will only be solved by continuous and open debate. We cannot leave decisions to governments or international organizations, because they can never be aware of particular circumstances. The standards of ethics and of science have been greatly improved for experiments on man by the introduction of local ethical committees. The cause of scientists, humanity and animals may be protected by the development of local groups which oversee proposed experiments on animals just as similar groups examine experiments on man.

Nor is ethical concern about the use of animals confined solely to a few 'pure' researchers. Though Beecham's witnesses seemed determined to remain free to test any product on animals, they have eschewed some of the most cruel experiments. They made clear to the House of Lords Select Committee their distaste for the two most controversial toxicity-testing procedures:

The LD50 test in its characteristic form implies dosing to an extent that will kill half the animals; and where the materials under test are essentially low in toxicity, as is obviously the intention with cosmetics, this would mean, if carried out in the classical way, a very large dose to the animals. In my view, this has no meaning in safety evaluation. It measures the ability of something to cause harm by gastric distension rather than by toxicity, and we are not interested in that kind of information. By giving a reasonable dose calculated to represent the greatest dose that the human is likely to encounter, we are obtaining useful predictive information, usually without the slightest effect on animals . . .

On the controversial and highly publicized Draize and LD50 tests, Beecham said that they did not normally put undiluted shampoo into rabbits' eyes, but used shampoos diluted 'to the extent that discomfort or stress is minimal', and noted that the *International Journal of Cosmetic Science* (1979, 1, p. 123) had published an account of this technique. They said they did not find it necessary to use the LD50:

Since 1968, to assess the risk of acute toxicity, it has been our practice to give a single dose, usually 5 grams of product per kilogram of body weight (e.g. to a rat). If there is no major effect, which is the usual result, no further testing is necessary. It is almost inconceivable that a human being could accidentally ingest a greater quantity pro rata to body weight.

They also said that non-animal methods are developing, and have the merit of consistency and cheapness.

Modern attempts at reform and the Halsbury Bill

In the decade from 1966 and 1976 there were no fewer than a dozen Private Members' Bills, none of which became legislation. In 1906 and 1965 there were major reviews of the legislation, some of which led to minor improvements in the administration of the Act.

Lord Halsbury was the President of the Research Defence Society (which promotes the usefulness of animal research, but also has sponsored some work on alternatives) when he published the Laboratory Animals Protection Bill in July 1979. The Bill represented the aspirations of the scientific society whose brief it is to defend and promote the serious usefulness of scientific research work, especially that requiring animals. But it was a sophisticated piece of work.

It must be said that in essence it remained a scientists' charter, and that the Committee for the Reform of Animal Experimentation, as the most striking campaigners for change, still had plenty of work to do – and still have.

The Halsbury Bill immediately underwent an extensive examination when research scientists, industrial scientists and welfarists all had their say in bending it towards their own requirements. It had mostly satisfied the scientists, and the discussions were mainly 'negotiations' between the pro-research lobby and the welfare lobby. At the end of the process in April 1980, the Select Committee of the House of Lords reported and published the Bill as amended.

Again and again, and especially in its discussion with the Home Office, the Select Committee came back, as everyone does, to the rarity of prosecutions under the Act: there have been none, directly under the Act and for contravention of its terms, 'since the very early days of the Act', said the Home Office. (People have often been admonished for their behaviour, and one or two people have had licences revoked following conviction for other animal-related offences.) The Home Office stressed that fifteen inspectors could work only by maintaining good relations with the researchers carrying out millions of experiments. The Chief Inspector had this to say:

As I see it, the fact that there are no prosecutions is in fact a mark or measure of the efficiency of the inspection. If there were many prosecutions, I would be beginning to think the inspectors were not doing their job. As I see their job, it is so to conduct themselves that their licensees do not in fact infringe either the conditions of their licences or the letter of the law. That, to my mind, is the job of the inspectorate. If we ever get into a situation where it is believed that the inspectorate is a police force, we will not need fifteen inspectors; we will need 1,500, because we will need one or two on every premises.

He thought that putting responsible people 'over an obstacle course' before they got their licences ensured that licensees would be responsible.

The Committee for the Reform of Animal Experimentation (CRAE, drawn from parliament, the welfare bodies and the scientific community, with Clive Hollands as its secretary) suggested that a new Act ought at the very least to have machinery for a later tightening-up of its provisions. They believed that:

1. Legislation should apply to any procedure involving interference with an animal's normal condition of well-being, where pain or distress is liable to occur, unless by a veterinary surgeon for purposes of diagnosis or treatment of a particular animal in the course of normal veterinary practice.

2. All animals being used for any purpose under the Act which has the potential for causing pain or distress must be kept under regular supervision. If, despite all reasonable precautions before, during and after experimentation, an animal is found to be suffering pain or distress, it must be forthwith humanely killed, and the procedure shall not be re-employed.

3. The regulations shall apply to the usage of at least the following classes of animals, including foetal and larval stages: Mammalia, Aves, Reptiles, Amphibia, all classes of bony and cartilaginous fish, as well as certain orders of the Cephalopoda.

4. All experiments should be open to scrutiny by trained animal welfare officers, and members of the Advisory Committee on Animal Experiments and persons appointed by them in addition to the inspectorate.

But, crucially, CRAE is also looking for a beefed-up advisory committee which could work on its own accord and be empowered and entrusted to make a fuss when it saw a need to. They noted:

There has already been an exchange of views between the present Home Secretary [William Whitelaw] and CRAE on the composition of the advisory committee, and there are some differences of view on the balance between scientists and welfarists.

This sounds like an understatement and a half. Certainly, CRAE's submission quoted the Home Secretary's reply to them:

Each of the members will need to have regard to the balance between the legitimate requirements of science and industry and the protection of animals against avoidable suffering.

The difficulty with that formulation is clearly that it may simply be the statement of the fact that any member acceptable to the Home Office would at least have to accept that science and industry were capable of having legitimate requirements in animal use, but that they must not be abused; or it might mean that the Home Secretary would only accept as possible members of the Advisory Committee on Animal Experiments people who were clearly thinking along lines closely proximate to the current standards (or, perhaps if the mix of interests were wrong, people prepared to live in a constant minority on an issue dear to their hearts).

The Research Defence Society claimed in their memorandium, quite frankly, to have been successful in 'frustrating several attempts to change it [the 1876 Act] in a manner that would have been detrimental to scientific research and public interest'. 'Don't I know it,' commented Lord Houghton. He wanted to know how the hostility between the RDS and the welfare groups could be overcome. Dr Uvarov, the RDS spokeswoman, said that she thought the Halsbury Bill was precisely of the kind to close the gap, and that it had engaged the support of people who had opposed the previous attempts to improve the 1876 Act. But the chairman of the committee,

Lord Ashby, tried to press the RDS on how the gap was to be closed.

You give as an example that British drug manufacturers in testing a drug used 698 animals. I think you can take it that it totals up to that. I did it with a computer. This is the acceptable price for an enormously important drug. This is all right. So far we are with you. Now I come to the point about closing the gap. Look at the top of the next paragraph: in order to introduce a new food colour you have used 1,740 animals. I put it to you that this is what the public is worried about, or one of the things, and if you are going to help us close the gap we would like to know what amendment you would like to see in the Halsbury Bill which takes account of the fact that a colouring matter needs 1,740 animals to get on the market and a drug, which many members of the public would readily accept, needs 698 animals. Do you see any possibility that we should propose amendments which would deter what one would call frivolous or inessential research which puts colouring matter into margarine?

And the reply from Mr J. D. Spink, on behalf of RDS (which was giving evidence for the Food Manufacturers' Federation) said that the important factor was the 'improvement of life' criterion, which the proposed new Bill suggested in replacement of the 1876 'alleviation of suffering' as a legitimate purpose. (This change in the law would be a blatant reduction in the protection given to animals: they could now be used to research things of simple convenience to people, rather than of real importance to them.)

It is clear that there are all sorts of ways of looking at what constitutes 'improvements of life', and in particular in food. Mr Spink, for example, said:

For instance, the toiletry-field people think of the testing of lipsticks and face powders and that sort of thing, but it also includes all the toiletries used for babies, where there is a great deal of skin sensitivity. It also, I think, probably includes the testing of contraceptives because I do not think you can embrace contraception in the alleviation of suffering as one of the authorized purposes, and I think that population control would be regarded as an improvement of life. But even when you come down to things like food additives, as I say we are not just talking about green dye in peas, we are talking about the whole subject of convenience foods. Not just dyes. There are stabilizers, emulsifiers, anti-oxidants and so on which go into foods and produce these convenience foods, which I think most housewives would accept have improved the quality of their lives by reducing their housework burden. So we are talking about something, as I say, more serious than is often appreciated.

[The chairman]: We take that point of course and we realize that, but I raised this because when it comes to closing the gap this is the sort of consideration on which we need help, and I think what you have said very courteously is that you cannot offer us any help.

[Mr Spink]: I am sorry.

The Beecham Group's witnesses, whom we have seen to be enlightened about the sort of experimental technique that they employ, nonetheless urged that there should be no distinction between classes of product: toiletries and cosmetics should be given the same treatment as medicines, and to do otherwise 'would prove both impracticable and against the public interest'. They said:

> In our opinion, to evaluate the safety-in-use of cosmetics and toiletry products, some animal testing cannot always be avoided without creating an unacceptable risk to human health. Nevertheless, we believe that the extent of testing done, when it is judged to be necessary, and the effects on animals of the procedures used are commonly exaggerated in the public mind.
>
> We do not see the distinction between one product class and another. If they are to be used by humans, if they have a free choice to use materials, then it is important, it is ethically necessary, that the humans should be assured that they are not likely to do harm. That would be the basic ethical defence.

They said that their own work on cosmetics or toiletries seemed to follow the pattern of the total of experiments on animals: that less than 0·5 per cent of experiments were for testing or researching these sorts of products, and that less than 5 per cent of their 240 licence-holders ever used procedures on animals for such work. Beecham's researchers were concerned that the delineation of types of research into medical and consumer-orientated products would not work well for the public interest. They cited sun-tan lotions which may turn out to be useful against skin cancer (which they claimed to be an increasing hazard in Western countries), and that products such as fluoride toothpaste and anti-perspirants have, or can have, a medical role, which makes the assumption that they are somehow always trivial a wrong one.

They said, and cited the exclusion of whale products as a case in point, that there was a constant need to be able to switch from one ingredient to another even in well-known products, and that that countered the view both that what was tried and tested need never again need testing and that we could stay within known boundaries in the product ingredients we used. (They also cited the change in oil-stocks from which detergents are made, and that over-tight control might send necessary research work abroad to laboratories where animals were treated less compassionately.)

The witnesses from Beecham believed that they could not do anything to invite public scrutiny of their work in this field:

Unfortunately, it is our practical experience in this country that to expose oneself individually leads to a high probability of damage on your property and threats to the personal safety of your staff. Therefore it would be correct to say that we are intimidated into remaining silent at the present time, unless we are able to behave collectively. The same criticism would apply to providing opportunities for the media to come and see what we do.

If this is true, then it is the most salient and damning point to be made against the activities of the animal activists. What they do in making the issue famous and loud (and the smoking beagles, which were a milestone in animal welfare history, were only revealed by their activities) is always close to being as damaging as it is valuable: that is their own moral dilemma which the brighter ones among them recognize well enough. The least the animal welfarists should do is not take a scientist's preparedness to discuss and reveal his work as anything less than something positive. To use it as a way of identifying and locating one's next target would be a shabby reward indeed for the few scientists who will put their heads over the parapet.

What to do now?

In May 1982, the unofficial text of the draft *European Convention of the Council of Europe for the Protection of Vertebrate Animals Used for Experimental and Other Scientific Purposes* was beginning to circulate. Proposals from the Select Committee, the Home Office Advisory Committee on Animal Experiments and the Council of Europe were littering the desks of welfarists and research defenders like confetti. They mostly wanted the animals looked after better both before and after their spell under knife or needle; they mostly tightened up the supply of animals to avoid pet-stealing; they mostly improved the sponsorship of applicants to do research; they (but not the European Convention) mostly extended the range of species to be protected.

But on the great issues of principle, none of them were prepared to accept that the nature of the debate on animal protection has changed and that, in common with matters ranging from euthanasia and other medical issues right through to the proper armaments or the sort of power sources which a nation might adopt, there has been developing an awareness that issues do now require to be discussed in detail by the public or, failing that, by people trusted by the public to be decent representatives of the public conscience and anxieties.

It is clear that no law could ever define what pain should be allowed to be inflicted on animals, and that the balance between public safety (whether protection from the trivial or serious consequences of the malfunction or misuse of trivial or valuable products) and the suffering of animals is one which will always be complex and which is only just now beginning to be discussed.

It is time that it was understood that no definition of pain or purposes is going to be good enough for everyone now, or even for many people now, and that no definition of them will stand the test of time. The only sensible law will be one which ensures that the Advisory Committee is empowered, both legislatively and logistically, and required to keep these awesome difficulties under review, and be seen to do so to the satisfaction of serious opinion.

A minister answerable to parliament for its administration should run the Act; but the Advisory Committee must be of the kind to make a considerable public fuss if it feels that the minister is failing in his proper scrutiny and care of the procedures by which animals are allowed to be tortured for man's advantage. The Advisory Committee would have to be widely drawn. There could be elections to it, and it could quite definitely know what was going on, and could give an account of what was actually happening, so as to allow proper debate.

The Department of Health and Security's witnesses to the Lords Select Committee went so far as to say that this sort of committee could work, and outlined something very like it. But what actually happened to this proposal, or guideline, which the chairman of the Lords committee called 'interesting and important'? The gist of the relevant section of the Halsbury Laboratory Animals Protection Bill, as amended by the House of Lords Select Committee, was:

1. The Advisory Committee shall be of not less than nine and not more than fifteen members, all appointed by the Home Secretary.

2. These people will have to be chosen from people who the Home Secretary thinks will help him administer the Act, and include people versed in science and in animal experimentation, and others qualified 'by their knowledge and experience of' animals;

3. The Committee shall advise the Home Secretary on any issue which he refers to them, and keep under review the use of animals in laboratories (including the purposes for which they are used) and how to reduce their numbers or suffering, while also being the Home Secretary's guide to public opinion on the Act.

4. The Committee will be notified by the Home Secretary if he intends to make changes in licences and be consulted on certain changes to how the Act is administered.

5. The committee shall make an annual report on its work, and the report should be put before parliament.

These provisions, combined with a new requirement for more detail in the statistics to be compiled by researchers which went some way towards making the annual statistical return less 'laconic' (as it had been described by the House of Lords Select Committee Report), look pretty good. But the amended Bill did nothing serious to tighten up the purpose to which animals might be put (they include very vague ones like 'the maintenance and enhancement of public health'), and it did little to help weed out the use of animals in painful or distressing ways. In short, it was exactly the kind of Bill which needed the back-up of a powerful committee, whose work would have to be detailed, serious, continuous and informed.

And that would, under the present Act, require a Home Secretary who (a) funded the Committee properly; (b) appointed the right mix of people to ensure that debate would be informed and not forever crippled by hopeless imbalance between the interest groups, or (what could easily also happen) exact equality between them; and (c) gave it much broader powers.

On this, where a new Bill can be definite, positive and clever, the amended Bill does nothing, and the Advisory Committee on Animal Experiments report does not even bestir itself to point out the inadequacy of the case. For many campaigners, including CRAE and in particular Richard Ryder, this remains the crucial issue. Ryder told the Select Committee that he believed that the Advisory Committee needed to be composed of 40 per cent each of 'users' and of welfarists, with the balance being held by a 20 per cent 'block' of lay public, in order to give the humanitarian voice its proper role.

Ethical committees are being introduced in many difficult medical and scientific fields, as much to protect scientific as public conscience. We should not deny the animals in laboratories the serious consideration which has been called for since the 1870s and is still refused.

4

ZOOS, CIRCUSES
AND WILDNESS

A lone seal darts around its circular pond, as regular as a tube train in its tunnel. An elephant pursues its ritual route behind its moat. A zebra, separated from its girlfriends for the day, patrols its side of the stable door, with its humbug-striped body as firm as a ballet-dancer's.

This is London Zoo on any day; and these are the sorts of images which some of us carry away from zoos, and which make many of us hate them. There is something bizarre and sad about wild creatures being kept in environments which are as far away in type as they are in distance from their real homes.

London Zoo is one of the oldest of the 'worthwhile' English zoos: there were serious ones in ancient China and elsewhere, and there were menagerie-style wild animal collections here long before the Zoological Society of London opened its gardens at Regent's Park in 1828. It is world-famous and well respected. It takes its work seriously, and its personnel certainly do care about the creatures in their charge. Yet London Zoo is £1 million in the red, with attendances down by over 20 per cent in the last year; it has had a government top-up of £1 million already and is hoping for more. The adult gate price is £3.50 (babies and toddlers free; fives and over, £1.50). Almost certainly it is recession and not the customers' burgeoning sense of the dignity of animals that has brought the zoo to this pass. But, ignoring the cause, it gives those of us who think that gawping at captive animals is bad for people, and that being captive is pretty galling for animals, something like ammunition.

Of course, with the smaller commercial zoos it is easy to

98

criticize them on simple grounds of cruelty: their financial shortages are endemic, and they do not have the back-up of expertise and resources with which to help their captives live even tolerably healthy and fulfilled lives. In recent years there has been an attempt to clean up the 150 or so zoos in Great Britain. Finally an Act was passed, the Zoo Licensing Act 1981, which proposed to institute a system whereby local authorities must inspect and license zoos, with a certain amount of authority remaining with a central panel whose powers have not yet been fully defined – indeed, the standards which the Act will set have also not yet been defined. But the Act will probably ensure that some of the worst excesses of cruelty and bad animal-housing of under-financed zoos will be curbed.

In 1978 Stefan Ormrod (now Chief Wildlife Officer at the RSPCA) and Bill Jordan (a vet who was with the RSPCA and now runs the People's Trust for Endangered Species), from personal experience which ranged from the best to the worst, wrote *The Last Great Wild Beast Show* to expose inadequate zoos. The story which they unfolded of the bad ones was horrifying indeed. They had come across badly run wildlife and safari parks (the drive-in zoos which some of the stately-home owners of Great Britain rushed to create, often in partnership with Jimmy Chipperfield of the famous circus family) and every kind of sadness in the shoddier commercial zoos. They named no names, except in praise, but a picture unfolded of a breed of zoo-owner or manager with precious little understanding of animals and a chronic shortage of capital. It seems that the zoo trade attracts a particular sort of maverick: they seem to be the sort who would have been big-game hunters had there still been sufficient business in that line. The resulting misery for animals ranged from monkeys sleeping in winter-flooding bunkers on the islands of one wildlife park to badger cages which had concrete floors so that the badger's innate digging behaviour was wholly unsatisfied.

On the backs of the zoos there thrives an unsavoury trade in wild animals which is often poorly regulated and many of whose dealers are regularly under suspicion for breaking the laws of the countries of origin and of 'consumption' alike.

WTMU (The Wildlife Trade Monitoring Unit), a British-based organization, monitors the trade in wild animals, while the Convention on International Trade in Endangered Species does its best to list and forbid trade in species at risk. But with corrupt or inadequate governments in many parts of the world, and with large sums of money at stake, the trade in wild animals is as hard to contain as the trade in arms or drugs. While many creatures in zoos are captive-bred (Anthony Smith in his *Animals on View* puts it at 70 per cent for London Zoo in 1977), there are several species for which this is not the case. Elephants, pandas, and bottle-nosed dolphins are all animals which are common in zoos and yet rarely breed in captivity.

In the late fifties, there were around thirty zoos in Britain. But during the sixties, according to Ormrod and Jordan, a further 100 were opened (Anthony Smith reported that thirty zoos had recently closed by 1979). This was the period of the wildlife and safari parks: places out of towns within motoring reach for their customers. Many of them were and still are idealistic wildlife collections. Philip Wayre was able to start the Norfolk Wildlife Trust (opened to the public in 1962) because his poultry business had been hit by disease and the compensation made a useful capital sum. John Knowles started Marwell Zoological Park in 1972 on the fruits of a successful poultry business. Twycross Zoo, founded by two pet-shop owners in 1963, became famous for its primates, and for providing the chimpanzees which have sold so much tea in the Brooke Bond television commercials. These are all run by dedicated animallovers and researchers. Marwell especially is often cited as a tonic to any jaded zoogoer's palate.

Lord Bath and Jimmy Chipperfield opened the Longleat Safari Park in 1966, and it spawned many others. The car-borne families of the sixties were looking for entertainment, and they found it at zoos of various kinds. Ormrod and Jordan reckon that there is an annual potential audience of 20 million for zoos. London Zoo's annual report for 1981 cites market research to the effect that one in seven British families contains at least one member who has been to London Zoo (the figure is one in four for the south-east) and that parents still seem to think that a visit to a zoo is an essential part of the children's education. People see zoos either as places of entertainment or as places of education, or perhaps a bit of both.

But are zoos proper entertainment? What do people learn in them that is worth knowing? Thinking about animals has made quantum leaps in the last few years. The pressures of animal welfare campaigners, of ethological awareness and of constant exposure on television, especially in wildlife films shot on location (or perhaps more properly, in habitat), have made us think about creatures freshly. We have lost the capacity simply to enjoy animals as oddities and objects of marvel and wonderment. We are stuck with wondering how they feel.

Even in the mid fifties, this was much less the case than now. For instance, David Attenborough, the presenter of the recent *Life on Earth* television series, was able to write a remarkably gung-ho account of one of his animal collecting expeditions in *Zoo Quest to Guiana*. He had been working on a television programme which showed animals from London Zoo:

> It seemed to us that the programmes would have been greatly improved if we had first shown on film an animal in the wild state, and then produced the same creature alive in the studio so that viewers could see it in more detail.

Zoo Quest became a television staple, and I don't know that there were many protests that there ought to be good evidence that the animals were enjoying their part in the affair before they were snatched from their own world and shipped across the ocean to become TV stars. Reading the book now, one is left with a feeling of discomfort that the plight of the trapped animals seems to have caused little or no sympathy from the huntsmen.

Attenborough's account of capturing a caiman is a *Boys' Own Paper* story of derring-do (and undoubtedly his work required a brave man, prepared to suffer almost as much as the beast for the cause of television). The men do battle with the caiman with 'its ugly black snout', and its 'long evil head projecting out of the hole, glaring at us malevolently with yellow unblinking eyes'. At first reading, twenty-five years ago, few would have much doubted a human's right to capture something which is ugly, evil and malevolent, and which was in any case a pest to the local Indians, who would have killed it if they had found it. Today we are not so sure.

And now we find David Attenborough on television still, and being quoted by the London Zoo's annual report for 1981 in BBC's *The Zoo: A Portrait of an Institution*:

It is essential that human beings should remain in touch with the reality of the natural world. You may say that with films and television and photographs people can appreciate what an elephant is like, but I don't think you can from print, or a television set; you have to see one, you have to appreciate the immensity of the beast, the smell that it makes, the noise that it makes, and that town-dwellers can do in zoos.

But there is just as likely to be a contemptuous familiarity about a visit to the zoo. Animals are seen there as dependent upon us and submissive to our needs. The animal is seen as part of our world and is palpably living as our guest at best, and more likely our prisoner.

Wild animals should be extraordinary to us because of the witness they bear that there do, just, still remain the sort of places from which we sprang as the brighter primate, and which we have, with our dangerous power, now rolled back into a few threatened corners. These are not just the wild places where we are the unwelcome guest or conquistador, the huge inhospitable regions of the world. In particular, they are the places where our destructiveness has not yet wrecked the vibrant life-forms which have evolved and survived alongside our own development, and which we now threaten.

The early big-game hunters did not know that they were attacking life-forms whose survival was a fragile thing: they thought they were pitting their courage (the best of them) against nature which was red in tooth and claw, and capable of surviving their depredations. And perhaps the early- and mid-twentieth-century zoological collectors were able to say that the creatures they were collecting were not then scarce. But now they have certainly changed their tune. The argument now is that since creatures are so threatened, either as potential food or by having their required habitats destroyed around them, it is essential that the few of some species which remain be gathered together in a rescue operation. The zoo has become the static ark, temporarily beached in the midst of a fee-paying public.

Modern zoos, sensing that the out-and-out peep-show approach will no longer do, have gone for the great worthiness. They describe themselves as being involved with education, conservation and research. They claim that people learn to love the brute creation which they see before them in zoos; that with wilderness under such threat, zoos may be the last refuge of threatened creatures; and that zoos can learn about animals, and especially about how to breed them in captivity.

Dr Brian Bertram is the curator of mammals at London Zoo. A born enthusiast and an expert on the animals of East Africa, it hurts him that anyone might have it in for 'good zoos, like London's', especially when more money would, he believes, mean that they could do a good job better. And June 1982 was a good time for him to take a sceptic into the mammal house, where he could show off a pair of glowingly bronzed golden lion tamarins, no bigger than skimpy kittens, and their days-old twins, clinging together in their Habitat-style little bit of jungle in an English city. There are fewer than one hundred of these little pieces of perfection in the wild. 'I wouldn't like a world in which there were no more of these little fellows,' says Dr Bertram.

Unlike most of the 600,000 species of plant and animal predicted as destined for the missing-presumed-dead list by the end of the century, these tamarins will have a place to live. Dr Robert Martin, an expert on primate evolution and no fan of the traditional zoo, is on the council of Gerald Durrell's Jersey Wildlife Preservation Trust. 'We have unleashed a holocaust on natural environments,' he says, and he accepts that captive breeding may have some small role to play, though he believes that only conservation reasons can justify keeping captive wild animals.

In summer 1982 London Zoo had babies galore: there were young of white rhino, the tamarins, pygmy hippo and gorilla, to name just the famous ones. But the southern white rhino is no longer the threatened creature it once was, since South Africa has managed to maintain several on reserves (though arguably what South Africa maintains may not be secure since a change of government is possible). In the case of gorillas, their intelligence alone makes them a worrying case for zoo conservation; however, so much effort is now being put into breeding them in captivity that it is at least possible that they will be allowed the kind of social life in the future that London Zoo's Guy never had. The tamarins seem like an almost benign piece of zoo maintenance: highly threatened at home, it does at least seem possible that they may have a tolerable life in zoos, provided that they are given environments which are not prison-like. But it remains to be seen whether London's pygmy hippo survives: the previous year's baby did not.

No one pretends that using zoos as conservation banks is easy. Though a high percentage of London Zoo's population is captive-bred, there is precious little comfort to be drawn from that. There is an enormous range of creatures among London's 633 non-domestic species of mammals, birds, reptiles and amphibians, and many of them either are not threatened or have large captive populations: lions and tigers, for instance, breed prolifically in captivity. Many more species do not breed easily in captivity but are relatively easy to obtain: zoo authorities reckon, for instance, that historically elephants have probably killed a keeper for every captive birth that has been managed.

Jonathan Barzdo, founder of the Association of British Wild Animal Keepers and a consultant on wildlife conservation, has taken figures from the London Zoo annual report for 1981 which show that the Zoo's recent record in maintaining populations of the really seriously threatened mammals is not good. Using criteria from the Red Data Book (RDB) of the International Union for Conservation of Nature, a world authority on the threatened extinction of wild animals, London Zoo had forty species of wild mammals in the Rare, Endangered or Threatened categories. Among these are chinchillas, which are rare in the wild but are farmed commercially for their fur, and Jamaican hutia, which are no longer rare in Jamaica. These two species did breed.

Their onager (a wild ass), scimitar-horned oryx and markhor did breed and some of their babies survived. But their polar bear, pygmy hippo and gaur (a wild ox) young did not survive. Out of their forty RDB species (four of which are kept in single-sex groups), eleven had babies which survived at least thirty days. But within the RDB species there were also thirteen deaths of animals over thirty days old (the figures only show pre- or post-thirty-day deaths). And so, taking that year's report, in London Zoo's total contribution to the maintenance of RDB species, there was a deficit of two animals. Of London's wild mammal species, 23 per cent were RDB-listed, but they made up only 3·24 per cent of the births.

If this was a representative year, the picture is not good. It leads one to say that in addition to the proposition that only conservation may be used as a rationale for a decent zoo, and then only with caution, there needs to be a very careful assessment of which creatures in captivity seem capable of reproducing themselves there, and a restructuring of zoos so that they devote themselves to giving 'target' animals the kind of lives which lead them to breed. This will be expensive, but it may also prove popular with a public which likes births in zoos (witness the excitement whenever Ching Ching the female panda is supposed to be pregnant, or the stunning increase in zoo attendance which attended the birth of a world-famous bear like Brumas in 1950 when, says Anthony Smith, attendances at London touched 3 million, as against less than half that now). It is very probable that zoos will soon come in for the kind of criticism that attaches now to battery farms or even research laboratories. They will be able to head it off only by adopting the kind of view that informs Gerald Durrell's Jersey Wildlife Preservation Trust, where no animals are kept merely because the public have got used to seeing such creatures.

But such an approach will require a reorientation for zoos and their public towards larger numbers of a particular species (to provide a sustainable group of mammals may need up to 200 well-matched individuals), and also, insists Dr Martin, a positive policy of field studies. Keeping animals in zoos requires more skill than we now possess (let alone more finance than we are prepared to devote), and certainly the reintroduction of captive wild animals into their natural habitat will often be as difficult as learning how to breed them in captivity has been.

The latest book of the distinguished American biologists and conservationists, Paul and Anne Ehrlich, *Extinction*, suggests that zoos and even small reserves will do little to conserve wild creatures and plants. The experience of British plant conservation is that it is possible to preserve a few individuals of a species in an environment which is sufficiently protected. The public will help to pay for that. But maintaining habitats – by which one means the naturally sustaining environs of a wild creature or plant – is a far harder and more daring target. It is also the prerequisite of there being any serious points in captive breeding.

The Ehrlichs quote Paul Ehrlich's letter to the USA Fish and Wildlife Service in 1980 on the desperate attempts to safeguard the Californian condor, in captivity if need be:

Even the most wildly successful captive breeding programme would be for naught if there is not sufficient habitat to support the birds after re-release ... the condor therefore should be preserved not just out of intrinsic interest, compassion and its own ecological role, but most importantly because it can serve as a rallying symbol for protecting large areas of habitat and thus many other endangered organisms.

But, as the Ehrlichs recognize, it is all too likely that any success with captive breeding will be taken in the opposite sense – namely, as an indication that wild state habitat is not needed. We could, it will be argued, have our rare species *and* the (temporary) usefulness of their habitat to our exploitative ends.

We are in the position at the moment of destroying habitat but trying to conserve species. There is a fair chance that we will be unable to do the latter. It is almost certain that whatever species we manage to conserve in captivity will over a few generations become a highly artificial version of what we set out to preserve. Already Przewalski's (Mongolian) wild horse is a creature somewhat unlike its forebears, and though it is cited as a species with either tiny or non-existent wild populations but with quite solid captive-bred numbers, it has started foaling, for instance, at times of the year that ensure that its progeny could only survive with difficulty in the wild if reintroduction were to be attempted.

But still we pursue the policy that conserving species is the first priority: we are using species as the signal of what matters in conserving naturalness and wildness on the planet. This policy carries with it the danger that we shall underestimate the value of wilderness simply *qua* wilderness. What is the point in having a few preserved, museum-state species when we have allowed all wilderness to be corrupted by human presence and depredation? We would be in the position of people who have maintained a nation's flag but eliminated the nation itself. Why keep a few symbols of wildness (tortured, genetically weakened and captivity-orientated, like recidivist human prisoners)? Why not instead put our effort into maintaining some wilderness lands, whatever their species content? This view assumes that a tract of Brazilian jungle is valuable whether or not it is also the habitat of some rare creature; or that an English woodland scene is important for its bluebells, quite irrespective of whether it is the last preserve of the last orchid in England. Better to preserve the jungle or the woodland as places which humans do not touch than to engineer them and manage them in such a way that some rare creature is preserved. Queen Victoria saw this when she asked that a piece of Kew Gardens be preserved as untouched: humans can do many things, but can they learn the sublime lesson of letting things be?

The Ehrlichs cite (with approval) the case of the Hawaiian goose, which after a world-wide campaign for its survival is now being bred in an ingenious way which seems to produce babies that are not fixated on humans (their parents are penned and flightless, but the young can fly off to the wild). However, it looks as though it is possible that the new wild population will need protecting from predators which have been introduced since the original and, in some cases, still-existent threats to their forebears. If these and other management needs are inflicted upon the habitat into which we introduce our captive-bred creatures, or upon habitat which we want to make more amenable to a particular species, in what sense have we pre-served nature? One cannot both farm nature and leave it undis-turbed. Rarity and the quality of being exotic can become too powerful as desiderata of our conservation policy: preserving wilderness – raw, untouched, unmanaged, unpopulated – might be a better one.

Jonathan Barzdo noted in his contribution to an ICA's zoo project booklet in June 1982 that there are about 800 captive Siberian tigers (more than there remain in the wild) which, it has been estimated, will cost around £22 million to maintain till the end of the century. Why not spend the money preserving a decent stretch of wilderness?

It will have to be a large place if it is not merely to be a kind of big outdoor zoo, a wildlife park in the home of wildlife. All the evidence goes towards the view that nature requires to be a spacious state: for the 200 tigers that might make a self-sustaining population, a simply immense, a probably imposs-ible, tract of land would be needed. It looks all too much as though there is now no real possibility of us leaving alone enough land to create a real wilderness environment for some of the animals we are interested in to live in, as though we and they were separate and not deeply enmeshed with one another's fate.

This approach will require the kind of forbearance that humans have never yet shown. It requires a passion for ecologi-cal values that communities and nations do not yet display. However, the government of Indonesia has said that it hopes to maintain a hands-off policy for some of its land-space: this is a signal.

Giving the second World Conservation Lecture in London in March 1982, Indonesia's Minister of State for Develop-ment Supervision and the Environment, Professor Emil Salim, said of his country's determination to pursue an 'eco-development':

To safeguard the biotic wealth that is our heritage, we must provide the genetic treasure represented by our fauna and flora with its appropriate and inviolate habitat.

Frankly, we lack the precise knowledge of what constitutes our own natural wealth and how to protect it. But we know that it must be preserved and at least, as a first step, be provided with areas where it can be left undisturbed.

As Indonesia can be subdivided into various ecological regions, we will take steps so that in each region at least 10 per cent of the ecosystem will be set aside. This will constitute sanctuaries that will remain untouched except as living laboratories for scientific endeavours.

Meanwhile, we have zoos. It is ironic that places which so travesty and distort their very wildness should be sanctuary to the refugees from the world's disappearing wilderness. What is worse, we, who have wrecked our own home and theirs, now torture the last shards of creation's previous immense variety rather than let them go into the extinction we have forced on them.

But zoos are replete with ironies. Some of them breed white mice for their snakes (and who is to judge the comparative value of their lives?), and buy day-old chicks from battery-hen farms. London Zoo buys ex-MoD surplus rats and mice from the chemical warfare research centre at Porton Down and reports that 'about a quarter of a million locusts and large numbers of blowflies, houseflies and mealworm were produced [in 1981] as food for mammals, birds and reptiles in the collection at Regent's Park'.

Just a shade more romantically, there are pandas who won't reproduce, and lions who reproduce so much that they're on contraceptives. There is a grim little addition to the Zoo's statistics of their collection, which includes the item 'Culled'. In 1980 there was a newspaper outcry that London Zoo had killed off three baby bears and was at risk of having to do so again. Zoo authorities say that not many animals are now culled. But certainly there have been reports recently from Continental zoos where surplus captive-bred animals are butchered; doubtless it goes on here too.

While zoo animals generally can expect to be treated for their illnesses in a way which can hardly happen in the wild, some-times the veterinary attention which they receive gives rise to at least a feeling of distaste. To save him having to travel, Jambo, Jersey's gorilla, is now electro-ejaculated, as we have seen on television. Many animals at London and elsewhere are now reproducing via artificial insemination. The system may deprive British Airways of the publicity which it gains from claiming that they 'pander pandas': Ching Ching may yet be artificially inseminated to save her travelling. If the modern Noah comes in the guise of an artificial-insemination man, we have some reason to suggest that we are violating nature even while we want to preserve and conserve it.

Dr Robert Martin believes that the capacity to breed and bring up young is at least an indicator of happiness and well-being in most animals. He thinks that some female gorillas which cannot bring up young are unable to do so because of stress, and not because of their inexperience and the absence of learning from peers as had been suggested. The evidence for this view is partly based on the fact that some previously inattentive females do suddenly appear to be able to rear their second or third baby: perhaps they have reconciled themselves to zoo life.

The chance to breed never came to the tragic Guy (who died, indirectly but surely, of the now forbidden destructive kindness of his sweet-feeding public). It seems to have come to the exquisite tamarins. But what of the Andean great condors, the latest pair of its extraordinary soaring vultures which London Zoo has tried periodically to breed since the nineteenth century? Often there's an egg, sometimes a chick. In 1982 a chick was born which survived, at last. We must hope that any new young Condor gets a bigger cage than its parents ever did. Their cage is as much use to them as a shoebox to Concorde, and one cannot quite forget it, especially since – breeding or not – these great birds are often very aggressive with each other and their eggs have to be artificially incubated and their chicks, such as they are, hand-reared.

But, then, what are we to make of what animals want? The Andean condor has as its natural habitat half the heavens: what can it make of its zoo home, a pathetic cage in which the thing can hardly take off, let alone soar? And the tamarin may be small and cuddly-looking, but what do we know of the joys and horrors of its life in captivity or the wild (which goes towards Robert Martin's plea for increased field studies of such animals)? Of the individual tamarin which is captured in the wild, we may be able to do some crazy sum in which its wild-state pains and miseries are assessed against those that it must endure in captivity, especially if its fate in the wild is to die, after a life which may have been nasty, is certainly brutish and is about to be cut short.

But what to say of the creatures that we breed from the first captured parents? All the miseries of the captive-bred tamarins are at our door. Without our intervention these creatures would not be alive. If we withdraw our support, they will die as surely as their parents would have. And everything about their circumstances is a product of human intervention.

It may well be that the world would be a lonely place without these creatures to keep us company. And it may be that we yearn to keep them alive as a token of the last remnant of the huge variety on the planet which we are eroding. But there is no means by which we can explain to the animal that its miseries have been imposed on it because its extinction would make us sad. The last golden lion tamarin on the face of the earth does not know that it is the last in a long line. It knows no more of our desires for it and our need for it than we know about it, and that is terribly little. Animals are mysteries: that is all that we know about them.

It is in some sense to honour that awareness that London Zoo no longer holds a chimpanzee tea-party, on the grounds that it does young audiences no good to see the chimps being made to behave like poorly coordinated humans. Besides, it requires a tremendous amount of love, affection and attention to make chimpanzees go through their paces, and zoo keepers, hard pressed in other ways, could not find the time to do it well. Moreover, there is an anxiety that a young chimp who becomes too interested in human beings will find life all the harder when adulthood looms.

In this respect, zoos are becoming rather self-consciously

superior about their former circus-like habits. But what of the circuses themselves?

There is a great tradition of circus life: it is one of the romances of childhood and of teenage life to run away and join one. Like visiting zoos and the sport of hunting, a trip to the circus is a custom which habit has made ordinary, and even wholesome. However, mostly because of campaigning by the RSPCA and its wildlife department, now run by Stefan Ormrod, there has been a change in public opinion. Around fifty local councils no longer allow circuses on their land, unless, that is, it is the Circus Hassani, run by one of the daughters of Coco the Clown, which uses no animal acts. The days of circuses which employ animals are now numbered: the public does not appear to like them as much as they used to, and it is harder every year for circuses to find the pitches which will make them money.

Beyond the preservation of a colourful way of life for a diminishing number of committed performers, there is nothing serious which can be said for circuses. They are entertainment pure and simple, if they are entertainment at all. Their animals are kept in small travelling cages while they are on the road, and subjected to training regimes which must at least occasionally, if not endemically, be cruel.

Of course, circuses deny that their training needs are cruel. Indeed, Robert Lacey, who in the winter of 1981 had a lion act with Circus Holiday, insisted both over the circus tannoy and in a tetchy private conversation after the show that his lion training had been done in the presence of an RSPCA inspector, whom he would not name. It would be strictly against the rules for an RSPCA inspector to endorse circus training of any kind (not least because the Society is committed to the banning of animal acts in circuses). But it is also the case that the RSPCA has had a good deal of difficulty in obtaining permission from circus-owners to watch their training sessions (quite aside from the near-impossibility of actually monitoring them effectively).

Mr Lacey's act seems to be typical of the kind of thing on offer. It is billed as an encounter between a wild beast and an unarmed man, symbolizing the toughness and dominance of the trainer over his submissive beast, but always with the frisson of pleasure that comes to an audience which knows that the immemorial ferocity of the beast may reassert itself, and Mr Lacey's head, momentarily interposed between the lion's upper and lower jaws, may be gobbled up. The skills which we are supposed to believe reside in the performer alternate between the powers to seduce or cow his adversary.

Still in the circus season of winter 1981, the grand old man of English circus, Dick Chipperfield Senior (brother of Jimmy, the safari-park man who is equally colourful) was involved in an Anglia TV confrontation with Stefan Ormrod (with whom he has often had well-publicized and good-natured but nonetheless entrenched contretemps on television) and a lady Tory councillor from Luton. Luton Council had just decided not to allow the circus on their land, and Chipperfield and Ormrod settled down to a routine row about whether or not some of the animals in Chipperfield's circus could conceivably have been captive-born as Chipperfield was claiming. It is a claim which goes towards letting circuses off the charge that they are plundering limited wild stocks of animals, but also – incidentally – it makes a nonsense, when true, of the full impact of the trainer's bravery. Chipperfield also insisted that everything in his circus was done by kindness.

'Look at me,' he said. 'I am an old man. I could not punch a hole in a cloud or box my way out of a wet paper bag.' (He speaks as a man who as a boy was nearly taken into care by the NSPCC because he was found going several rounds with a pugilist at a fair. His aunt had great difficulty in persuading the kindly child-defenders that nothing on earth could have stopped him boxing. He now believes that the RSPCA is similarly misguided in its protectiveness.) 'You're not saying that I would go into a cage with dangerous animals and frighten them, are you? When they're trying out a new young trainer in America, they send for me to pull him out if anything goes wrong; I can't do something like that using fear. Can I go in and beat up six lions?' Later, over drinks, he claimed to have pulled three trainers from the ring, saving them from maulings. And in saying it he undoes himself, with an engaging disingenuity: presuming the lions to be tormented beyond endurance by their

trainer to have risked attacking him suggests that though Dick
himself may be *simpatico* with the beasts, at least these three
trainers were not – though one might argue that for once the
lions were enjoying themselves in assaying a new form of
dinner!

Dick Chipperfield proudly says that though 'they've had a bit
of bark off me', his career has been remarkably free of damage
from his animals, though others fared much less well. He said
his son, Dick Chipperfield Junior, has 'had far more maulings
than me'. It is patently obvious that Dick Chipperfield loves his
animals, and entirely possible that he has a good understanding
with many of them: he will only allow that Hungarian gypsies
and their bears have a closer relationship with their animals or
can get more from them. He says he has trained a tiger to ride on
the back of an elephant, which must amount to an achievement
even if a cruel one. And he says that part of the training of lion
cubs relies on a trick which lionesses have of leaving their
young under a tree in a sort of fixated state until the mother
returns; an accomplished trainer draws on the instinct. But then
Stefan Ormrod said during that TV encounter that Dick's
appreciation of the ways of wild animals is highly coloured.
According to Ormrod, Dick asserted confidently in a previous
television appearance that elephants could perform tricks like
standing on their heads because it is what they sometimes do in
the wild (no talk then of the blocks and tackle and the goadings
and the use of the power of other elephants, with which it is
more normally supposed they learn such tricks).

He is so nice and serious a man that it is hard to enjoy
suggesting that the results of the attentions which he lavishes
on his animals – their performances in the ring – are not ennobl-
ing to them or even to him. Indeed, he gets very cross, perhaps
rightly, when people suggest that animals have anything like
dignity to lose. He thinks such talk is 'degenerate' and a sign of
ill health in society.

Dick Chipperfield is the kind of amiable propagandist that
journalists love. The *Observer* colour magazine ran a little interview with him on 20 December 1981 in which he celebrated the
fact – as he believed it to be – that his circus animals have bigger

brains than animals in the wild or in zoos. He believed it to be because he and his wife hand-reared their animals very often and spoke to them constantly. This is all very well, but it does nothing to wean a complacent public away from the dreary pleasures of the circus, such as they are, or to invite them to consider the less attractive side of circus life.

It is not because we know that animals suffer when they live in small cages on the road or endure (and perhaps sometimes enjoy) training that one condemns circuses with animals. It is simply because we do not know either way, and want to give the animals the benefit of the considerable doubt.

This does not seem to occur to another circus propagandist. The famous vet, David Taylor ('the finest veterinary surgeon in the world', says Dick Senior), is retained by the Association of Circus Proprietors (as he is by the commercial zoos organization) and is often cited by them as witness to the well-being of their animals. What David Taylor endorses, however tacitly, must be good for animals. Mr Taylor represents their respectability. In an interview printed by Austen Brothers' Circus about their animal care, David Taylor said:

In my experience, animals in the circus are very healthy, certainly as healthy as the animals in zoos and safari parks. Circus animals have no occupational diseases . . .

He added that lions are naturally lazy and that their working day of perhaps twenty-five minutes rather suited their temperament. Moreover, they are spared the predations and ill health which kill around 75 per cent of lion cubs in the wild. He went on to say:

The animals at Austen Brothers' Circus are certainly kept healthy, using the most up-to-date veterinary knowledge and equipment. It would be indulging in anthropomorphism to suggest that an animal was happy or unhappy. You can't ask a camel or an elephant how they're feeling today. But based on my own knowledge of animal behaviour in the wild and in captivity, and on evidence such as blood-pressure tests, I would say they are very contented with their lot.

However, it does seem that animals no less than people are capable of boredom and frustration. But then these experiences might have other and more positive corollaries: animals are apparently also capable of enjoying quite difficult tasks. Faced with a life in cages, it may well be that many animals quite enjoy that part of their day when they are up and doing, even if it is in a circus ring. Our difficulty is that we do not know anything about this pleasure and that we do not need to take the risk. Moreover, many of the performing animals that we appear most to enjoy watching are precisely those creatures about whose needs we have terribly little evidence: whales and dolphins, for instance, are clearly very bright, and perhaps have a great capacity for suffering, yet they are prized tricksters, and the stars of at least eight dolphinaria in the UK.

Whatever we call the behaviour of animals kept in captivity, and especially in close confinement in boring surroundings, it is often not what ethologists might expect to see in the wild. Marian Dawkins cites Meyer-Holzapfel, Hediger and Desmond Morris, who all wrote in the mid sixties on the subject of the behaviour of animals kept in captivity. There are countless stories of bears in particular pacing endlessly in one route behind the bars of their cage or the perimeter of their enclosure. Some animals bought by zoos from circuses exhibit the phenomena graphically known as weaving and rocking: they often perform these movements for hours, sometimes rooted in one spot, in spite of their new-found freedom to move about.

During a visit to Sir Robert Fossett's circus last year, one could pay to see off-duty elephants, which swayed rhythmically together in their cavalry-style 'lines' under a marquee. On Christmas Eve, one of Robert Fossett's elephants – one of several who became frightened at the echoing noise inside Manchester's Belle Vue circus arena – pushed over a barrier and injured five children (apparently, none of them seriously). It was a sharp demonstration that animals are not predictable, however tractable they seem. There are to be no more circuses at the venue, which is being redeveloped. It ended nearly 150 years of zoo and circus life at Belle Vue, and probably none too soon.

Much of the behaviour of captive animals is bizarre in the extreme. A gorilla was observed to be vomiting and then studying its vomitus; it was suggested that this behaviour might have been to relieve the creature of boredom. Animals which are deprived of their normal behaviour patterns appear to indulge in a variety of aberrant stunts: they may be aggressive towards other animals, defecate and make games with their faeces, masturbate, or damage themselves (birds sometimes pluck their own feathers). Monkeys often seem to extract some sort of satisfaction from discomforting their keepers or audience by whatever means at their disposal. A zoo authority mentioned that elephants cannot be let out in places with loose stones, since they might throw one at a visitor. Desmond Morris reports monkeys who bit themselves so hard that they screamed out with pain.

In view of some evidence which suggests that animals, once habituated to captivity, seem to prefer it to a more adventurous life (*pace* human recidivists), there is no comfort to be drawn from an animal's demonstrated preference for its cage.

None of these peculiar pieces of evidence that captivity – let alone any direct cruelty in their training or management – strikes some animals badly will necessarily reveal themselves in lank fur or a dulled eye. They can easily be hidden inside a plump, sleek body which appears to be thoroughly hale. However, the creature could still be mad, neurotic or miserable.

We do not have to believe that animals and humans share every characteristic under the sun to be able to remember that human prisoners do not *look* obviously much affected by their incarceration. But we know that they are not happy (unless habituated and made gaol-dependent, which is hardly a condition we want to encourage). And the one great difference between animals and humans that we do know about goes towards our having a clear requirement to be doubly respectful of them: it is that we cannot find out from them what they want or feel.

5

PESTS, PETS AND THE PURSUED

Animals do not come in neat categories. The pet and the pest, for instance, can be the same animal seen through different eyes. One person pursues an animal with hounds, another with a lens; one person's prey is another's prized photograph. The animal which brings out in one an ancient bloodlust is an essay in tranquillity to another. For some people a bird is a unique individual; for others, something to be ticked off a list in a bird-spotting manual.

Just as pollution is often a case of too much of a good thing in the wrong place, so an animal can be transformed from a 'friend' to an 'enemy' according to its place and numbers. Furthermore, many species of animals are not as fixed in their own lifestyle, behaviour and relationship to humans as we may think. Not merely is any animal perceived differently by different people, but many animals are capable of developing very different sorts of ways of getting their living and 'satisfactions' within the course of their lifespan.

Cats, like foxes and many other mammals, are proving more variable and adaptable than was once thought possible. Their ranges vary between 200 acres and a twentieth of an acre. Nor are they the solitary characters of fiction: they seem to form rather well-structured societies, and not all merely what Dr David Macdonald of Oxford University calls 'unstructured aggregations around the milk churn' as was often thought. Among their studies of carnivore societies, Macdonald and his colleagues have found evidence of cooperation in farm-cat societies. Females, for example, may share in the task of rearing kittens, suckling one another's offspring in a communal nest.

They do not spend their time idly scrapping among themselves when they leave the uptight world of the backyard and the human family; instead they form complex bonds between groups of up to thirty individuals.

The feral cat is a sharp reminder that the animals which live most closely with us are in an important sense still absolute strangers to us, often maintaining a capacity to establish lives in which human company is rare or non-existent. The wild and the tame, the domestic and the primordial, reside more closely together than we think. Animals live among us, and not always out of choice; but they remain very different from us, however 'loving' the expression in a dog's eye, or however 'devoted' the housecat.

Cats are famously enigmatic. Often it is almost impossible to tell feral from tame. Many farm-cats in remote rural districts are hardly seen in the summer months, virtually living wild. In the winter, they become farmyard creatures again. A previous chapter looked briefly at what the proper names might be for the relations between people and animals. Whether a cat feels affection, devotion, familiarity or cupboard love towards its human companion, or merely likes the sensation of being groomed and the ease of feeding, is wholly unknown and perhaps unknowable.

Behind these enigmas there lie real difficulties in knowing what our obligations to animals might be. Many people are now seriously trying to establish what their proper attitude to various animals ought to be, and often seem to oversimplify what is possible in our defending the freedoms of animals, while even more people are prepared to see them trivially abused. The separateness of animals from people has become, especially in combination with the threat to wildness which we see all about us, a very potent source of curiosity and excitement to the human species.

Certainly, even being loved or admired by human beings is no guarantee for even their most cherished creatures that they will be well treated. Student demonstrators did not shrink from throwing darts at police horses in London in the early seventies and, more recently, the IRA blew up several horses (and their riders) in a London park. We continue to take our animals into whatever sorts of wars are going on at the time. There was a period when it was thought that dogs might be used in the recent Falklands conflict as mobile mine-detectors; only their probable inefficiency spared them.

We can take various lessons from such incidents, one of which is that we ought not to sentimentalize about animals at the expense of being indifferent to people: the policemen, troopers and infantrymen (the last presumably are now at greater risk because the dogs were found to be inadequate mine-detectors) concerned in each of the news stories could not be guaranteed as much coverage in the press as the animals. And that in itself is perhaps an example of the public's recognition that an animal's involvement in our human confrontations is always essentially 'innocent', or at any rate free of deliberate choice, in a way that few people's involvement can ever be.

It is also a good example of our peculiar sentimentality about animals; and 'sentimentality' here is precisely intended to mean the kind of indulgence in lazy emotion which springs so easily, and about equally, from anthropomorphism and misanthropy.

If some animals are put at risk of death at the hands of their human colleagues or their antagonists, many others are slaughtered for our own convenience. The RSPCA annually kill tens of thousands of unwanted or ill animals, the toll across the last six years being over a million individuals, leading to the accusation that they spend more effort defending people from animals than the other way round. The Old English Sheepdog Club has to have a sanctuary for the breed-members which attract owners (mostly because the breed looks so good in paint advertisements) but cannot keep them.

Other unwanted animals are less fortunate. Many horse markets receive rustled animals; but much of their business in horsemeat for the Continent comes from families fed up with, or unable to afford to keep, their children's ponies – and not always because the animal is too old for work or in poor health. The treatment of horses in transit and at market remains one of the saddest and most chronic abuses of animals.

Perhaps it should not shock us that the devotion surrounding the early days of many animals seldom attends them in their dotage. But there was surprised outcry in the press when it was revealed a couple of years ago that retired police horses also end up being eaten by Frenchmen, even after service at the sharp end of rioters. There was a feeling among many people that such horses deserve an honourable 'retirement' after their years of 'service'. But such a view does not take any account of what we may well assume to be the cardinal difference between animals and humans in regard to death: that we dread it, whereas they are usually presumed not to think along such lines. Death is something that most of us want to delay. Does an old police horse have the awareness of the notion of death which is the sole prerequisite of being able to dread it? Is the knacker, with his quick deliverance from the miseries of old age, so bad a person? I well remember the card of a local knacker's yard pinned to a farmyard wall: 'Old favourites painlessly destroyed'. The farmer in question – probably most farmers – would have chosen his knacker more carefully than any of his tradesmen. He was a scrupulously caring man, even if he was not inclined to run a sanctuary for his superannuated horses.

Some of the damage done to animals is not by mistake or because they are surplus to requirements. It is in some sense deliberate. It is done in the cause of making animals more perfect. Dog lovers have bred chronic disabilities into many types: dachshunds with bad backs, basset hounds with arthritic legs and a risk of glaucoma, great danes with a life span of just nine years, and many pedigree types with severe problems of aggressiveness. And dog lovers, despite veterinary opinion, lop the tails of many breeds.

Some of the people who 'love' animals most, and who need them most, are poor guardians, pets being killed by the 'kindness' of overfeeding being typical victims. There are occasionally very bizarre situations, as when, in Hackney recently, a couple were found living in indescribable filth among fifty-odd cats in their flat. They never let the cats, many of whom were diseased, out of doors. I have spent a couple of years writing every day in a room which overlooks a window through which I can see a pale old man in an undecorated room. He tends several cats and feeds the local pigeons, some of whom become trapped in his kitchen for days on end. Or are they trapped? There is no fluster as the man, the cats and the pigeons share their insalubrious world. It would take a cleverer moralist than I to have the smallest idea of whether what the man was doing was good or bad.

The urban environment of Hackney, where I live, is no more free of violence than any other 'natural' habitat. People have recently helped their dogs to gain access to the animal enclosures in Clissold Park, whereupon they savaged several of the deer there. And a Hackney cat or pigeon must beware of some streets, where groups of children with airguns take potshots at any small creatures.

There is a special order to the cruelty imposed by people when it is either careless or deliberate. There must be a great toll in animal misery imposed by formal, expensive, organized hunting, in spite of the codes which exist, and clearly people must make their own mind up about the traditions and rituals which might make such cruelty almost decent. The children and the not-so-young who terrorize wildlife with their airguns, crossbows and catapults do untold damage, and do it with perhaps a particularly base brand of malice.

For years now the papers have reported animals so killed, or surviving with pellets, bolts and arrows in them. Cats and hedgehogs have been reported in the past year as having been plunged into paraffin and burned, or bludgeoned to death, by youngsters. Animals have always had to bear the brunt of people's occasional exploration of the dark side of their nature. Part of the problem with any sort of hunting, even that for which people dress up, is that it may merely be the respectable, entrenched, ritualized version of the child with the burning cat. Stripped of its theatre and its pseudo-rationale, is it anything more?

If people are not the tidily rational beings that many reformers would like them to be, that may be a fact of their nature, just as they are sporadically also very generous. We condemn the boy with the burning cat for employing exquisite torture on an animal which is not merely innocent but which, but for the boy, would not have to expect anything like that sort of suffering. The fox is not precisely in that position in relation to the hounds, though people will differ greatly as to the degree of the difference and how much it matters.

Human beings, rational creatures that we are, do some very peculiar double-thinking about the cruelty that we impose on animals. We condemn, rightly and loudly, the people on the Broads who crucify swans on trees, or bend coat-hangers into a kind of shepherd's crook and swoop down in boats upon the birds so that they can catch one by the neck and tow it along behind (both of which have been reported recently). But it has taken years of gradually accumulating evidence, each irrefutable instance and piece of data piling upon the last, to build any kind of public feeling against the wholesale poisoning of swans by the lead from fishing tackle.

It is estimated that 250 tonnes of lead go into British rivers every year from anglers. It deceives swans into thinking that it is the grit they badly need for their digestive system, though its effects are actually miserable debilitation and ultimately death. There would be no difficulty at all in replacing lead weight by non-toxic equivalents. But nobody has yet passed this sensible law.

Such a law would not resolve the fundamental cruelty of fishing, which is one of the largest areas of self-deceit by the British public. If the occasional fox must endure being the brunt of tradition, how much worse is the plight of the far commoner fish, whose death throes, and even potential for pain, receive scant recognition or sympathy from the millions of fishermen in the country.

Perhaps because they live in a hostile medium and perhaps because they have cold blood (and also perhaps because they do not have hair or fur, legs, or appealing eyes) fishes are regarded as creatures which do not feel pain. But also we know that fishing is overwhelmingly the sport of the poorer people in society. It constitutes for many of them their main contact with the countryside. It is a prized solace and their passport to the rural outdoors. They are not ideal targets for radical reformers. But that does not make fishing the less cruel.

The truth is that, as the RSPCA-sponsored (but independent and expert) Panel of Enquiry into Shooting and Angling (1976–9) found, fish appear to fulfil much the same physiological criteria for experiencing pain as we do. As the Panel's secretary, Bill Jordan, noted:

> The evidence certainly was that a fish's mouth can feel pain. And what was even more shocking, perhaps because one didn't expect it, there was evidence that a fish's scales are covered by a sensitive membrane. They are probably in terrible pain while they are being handled, and often develop sores and fungi once they've been handled out of water.

We often ignore what we know about animals if it threatens to inconvenience us. Often enough, of course, our knowledge about animals and their ecology is painfully inadequate. Almost everything that goes on between us and animals is based on prejudice and myth, rather than on a firm foundation of knowledge.

The fox is a classic case of many of the problems, and is a perfect example of a clutch of ecological principles which are gaining ground in the public consciousness and which will radically alter our attitude to the wildlife around us. A recent fox-watch found that there were at least a couple of thousand foxes in Greater London, and they have even been seen in Trafalgar Square. David Macdonald has been studying the foxes of Oxford and the surrounding country for several years. He says that they can be found in any city environment, from the suburban garden owned by an elderly couple who leave much of it untended, right through to warehouses and derelict bomb sites.

As David Macdonald mentions in one of his papers, the modern urban dustbin is richer in food waste now than ever before, and less polluted, as it would seem from a fox's point of view, by cinders. Foxes are making themselves at home in the towns, and they may even be smart to the distinctions to be found among households. Some families regard the fox's appearance in the garden as cause for alarm, and others (probably the majority of those who know about their visitors) with pleasure. Yet others – probably the majority of those with foxes living close to them – have not the slightest idea that they have foxes around at all.

But it is not merely the fact that foxes adapt well to towns which is so fascinating. David Macdonald's work suggests that foxes are not divided between those that are townies and those that are ruralists. Some foxes live in the country and commute to the town to feed; others work the other way around. And foxes will change their predilections between the two; individuals are not necessarily fixed in their preferences. The fox, in common with many other mammals, is an opportunist: the town is just an environment where there is food to be had.

The flexibility of some animals, their resourcefulness and their ability to live alongside people have rather good-natured implications for our attitude to nature. While some people put naturalness on a pedestal, and renounce humanity and its works in an attempt to discover something pure and untainted, the fox has no such reservations. Moreover, other modern work suggests that much of our wildlife seldom conflicts with us.

It is true that some species have an alarming habit of thriving all too well at our expense. They are commensal with us, and good at taking crumbs from our table; at times they seem about to take the very bread from our mouths. The rabbit, for instance, introduced to this country probably in the twelfth century, can take a mighty toll in farm and garden produce. It was often introduced on islands by mariners in order to constitute a kind of dietary lifeboat for shipwrecked sailors, and it often bred and fed to the point where the populations of indigenous species were seriously affected.

But in this country they find plenty of food from farmers, and were therefore – almost certainly on purpose and brutally – introduced to an even more powerfully reproductive organism, myxomatosis, which still kills thousands of them. They are still sometimes an agricultural nuisance, and will certainly be much hunted.

People feel little pity for the shot rabbit, and yet less for the poor brown rat, an eighteenth-century introduction. Millions of these creatures live commensally with us, but they are our most feared animal enemy. They inhabit our houses, sewers, factories and barns, have a ferocious breeding capacity and a tremendous adaptability. One of the few people actually to admire these creatures is the Rentokil researcher who keeps several hundred of them in wild colonies around his research laboratory. Devoted to their elimination, he is an expert on their lifestyle. The control method that he must use is not the one he would like: because so many rat populations live where people and pets can devour the bait, most rats are now killed by a poison which means that they must endure internal bleeding until they die; often it will be a very slow death. Previously, they were killed by a poison which reliably sent them into hideous, but usually shortlived, convulsions before death.

We conduct our warfare against rats in town and country with hardly a second thought. Our renowned sentimentality for beautiful, intelligent, resourceful creatures stops short at these exemplars of the magnificence of Creation. They are just too prolific for their own good, too bound up with our dread of disease and too dependent on living at our table.

But the relationship between modern Britons and our wildlife is not often by any means a matter of resolving serious conflicts: sport, fun, sadism, admiration, sentimentality, commerce, all play their different parts and shelter under exotically contrived rationales put forward by animal 'defenders' and their opponents.

'I know many huntsmen,' said George Bernard Shaw, 'and none of them are ferocious. I know many humanitarians, and they are all ferocious.' That was in his introduction to *Killing for Sport* (1914) by Henry Salt, the excellent vegetarian and erstwhile master at Eton, whose *The Nursery of Toryism* (1911) never quite did deal the death blow to that school, any more than he got hunting outlawed.

A great tribe of rational people have tried to stop their fellows from dressing up in red coats and chasing about the countryside in pursuit of loopy dogs and the beautiful fox. The anti-hunt brigade has been as richly dotty as the hunters, and the rest of us have let them get on with their battles, believing that, very roughly, they deserved one another. But things are hotting up. Last year saw a watershed in the anti-hunting campaign: the Conservative Anti-Hunt Council is now on the march, matching the Liberals and the Social Democrats, and the left-wingers who always thought that the fox hunt was a clear case of the oppression of the working class.

The committed on either side have not always troubled to consider what effect hunting has on the country's foxes. We know extraordinarily little about the wildlife which comes to our farm fences and suburban doorsteps. But we do know more than we used to, and most of it gives us evidence for the view that hunters and anti-hunters are about equally ineffectual in influencing the fox population's quality of life.

There are two great difficulties with any argument about hunting as a method of controlling foxes. The first is that it appears that fox hunting has no effect whatever on the overall number of foxes surviving to the spring. And the second is that there is no evidence that foxes in general need controlling.

Wild animal populations very seldom need culling. The few wild animals that regularly reproduce and survive in the embarrassing numbers which cause man any trouble are often 'introductions', like the rabbit or rat, though the foreign mink appears to have found a stable niche. The fox, however, is indigenous to the country, and its population is maintained by a reproductive cycle which ensures in the summer (when there are around 500,000 British foxes) about four times as many youngsters as can survive the winter's dearth of food. Food supply, not predation, controls fox populations: the absence of voles, not the presence of hunts, is what stops a fox explosion. The fox never was a victim of other predators, even when there were wolves about: now people are its only, mostly unnecessary, animal enemy.

Indeed, someone who kills a fox sometimes merely creates a spare piece of territory for another fox, presenting an itinerant animal with an unexpected home-range.

Fox hunts are, however, reckoned to be quite efficient at

picking out weaker fox individuals: 'Most good fit foxes which give us a hard run will get away from us,' says Ian Coghill, the British Field Sports Society's conservation spokesman. If he's right, the foxes which his Worcestershire hunt catches and kills would probably have been among the majority which would not have survived the winter (or hunting) season anyway. He claims also that no one knows how much of a problem foxes would be in the winter, when their wild prey is scarce, because hunts, among others, have always played a part in keeping the populations lower just *before* the winter's severity than would otherwise be the case.

However, most farms have foxes near them, and few suffer fox depredations. It appears that very few foxes indeed bother to take lambs or chickens from their human neighbours. There is evidence that nearly all the lambs which foxes take are already dead: easier, the argument goes, for the farmer to blame the fox than bear the implied criticism of poor husbandry.

'Scrutator', a noted mid-nineteenth-century fox-hunting writer, said forthrightly that he thought that foxes were little trouble to poultry. 'If a farmer complained to me of a fox visiting his hen-roost, I gave him directions to shoot him, if he could, well knowing he [the fox] must be a cur or mangy.' In Cleveland there is a farmer's wife who has used foxes to keep the rats in check on her farm; they left her free-range hens quite alone.

Certainly, whether or not the fox which is a nuisance to the occasional sheep farmer is an aberrant animal, there are complications which surround aspects of fox 'nuisance'. Clearly, a vegetarian is free to say that sheep farming is itself an intrusion upon nature, providing an artificial source of competition between the fox's interests and ours. How much more severe those difficulties might be if there was a wholesale return to free-range poultry keeping is impossible to say; but certainly there will be many who would rather see the occasional 'criminal' fox chicken-taker itself killed, rather than the chicken farmer return his birds to a battery. But this is a hypothetical case.

There is a peculiar, more realistic, flipside of the coin. There is a decent logical space for the argument that pheasants, even if artificially reared and therefore to some extent an unnatural example, do need protecting from foxes, which will sometimes raid entire pheasant nests, sitting hen and all. After all, though the pheasant is hunted, and that incurs disapproval from some, at least this hunting provides a source of food for people. They may, of course, be people who are already well fed (though the great waterfowling shoots in Norfolk fifty years ago used to provide whole villages with food). A vegetarian is free to say that it is unnecessary food. But presumably there is a greater decency attaching to hunting an animal for fun and for food than to merely hunting it for fun.

The protection of species which we want to preserve for our own sport and food has led to massive and wrong-headed slaughter of predators in the British countryside in the past. Many gamekeepers annihilated birds of prey, for instance, in order to protect their masters' grouse on the moorland. They did not then know that even hen harriers, around a third of whose diet is grouse chicks, take around 7 to 8 per cent of a season's grouse offspring. This is well below the number that affects overall grouse populations across the seasons, though it may to some insignificant degree reduce the numbers of grouse available for shooting. Had the gentry known that their shooting was so little impoverished by predators, they might have stopped several of them being shot to extinction in Britain and others being severely reduced. But they did not, and even now there are many people in the country who do not understand it and continue to break the bird-protection laws rather than kowtow.

We may now realize that 'punishing' hen harriers for having a small effect on grouse numbers is ridiculous. But the case where an individual fox is clearly identified as a 'criminal' predator of lambs, hens or partridges would be a very different affair.

It is almost certain that in this country around ten times as many foxes die by shooting, collision with cars and monstrously cruel snaring as by hunting. There is clearly an important percentage of foxes roaming the country in dire pain caused by human beings; at least the fox hunt seldom causes injury, only a more or less untimely death, and might often be delivering a *coup de grâce* by killing an already injured animal. This leads to the speculation that those atavistic yahoos stampeding about on horseback, though conceivably loathsome in their bloodlust and in presuming to judge better than nature or God which foxes should die each winter, are actually the best of some fairly awesome evils, though many country people resent their intrusion on their land and tranquillity.

True, one might educate snarers and shooters out of their exaggerated anxieties about foxes as predators on game birds (though since some foxes do prey on some game birds, that would not be easy), and one might make country people desist from earning the few pounds which a fox pelt is worth, but none of these activities would be anti-hunt at all. They would, however, argue for a wholesale reappraisal of our wildlife, and certainly many of the fox arguments apply to badgers, seals, deer and birds.

It is clear that we need all the ecological insights that we can come by in our relations with 'pest' species. Should rabies ever come to this country, there will be major difficulties with our fox population, since it is so intertwined with the human population. Foxes are the commonest carriers of rabies on the Continent, and as the occurrence of rabies in animals comes nearer and nearer to the Channel and North Sea, naturally people become increasingly interested in the progress made towards finding a means of containing the disease. It now seems that live vaccines can be developed and fed to foxes via chicken carcases, and that the vaccines will not themselves be infectious, and will not therefore be dangerous promoters of the disease in their own right. But the work has not been conclusively proved to be both safe and effective.

The fox is killed for doubtful reasons and with doubtful effects: its interests and ours are seldom at odds. However, two other animals, badgers and seals, both of which are much admired by animal 'lovers', are regarded as being in competition with us. They are both attractive creatures, and they are both associated with diseases which assail animals which we use for food: the seal is a carrier of codworm, which reduces the profitability of some codfish, and is said to compete with us for fish; and the badger is now strongly, if circumstantially, implicated in the infection of cows with bovine tuberculosis in certain areas of the country.

It is notoriously well known that both seals and badgers are killed in an attempt to remove their nuisance value in certain circumstances. They are ecologically very different cases, though they are united in drawing an unprecedented hail of abuse from the press, TV and public upon the government-sponsored control schemes.

The badger is an unfortunate animal in that, like cows and people, it can be infected with bovine tuberculosis. But the fact that it can have the disease brings it into conflict with us. The incidence of bovine tuberculosis in badgers has a high correlation with the now very limited occurrence of the disease in cattle (mostly in the south-westerly peninsula of Britain), and therefore (since it has been proved under experimental conditions that badgers can pass their tuberculosis to cattle) the occurrence of the disease in badgers and cattle is now officially presumed to be more than coincidental.

The evidence is circumstantially damning. Where there are major outbreaks of bovine tuberculosis in cattle, there are often major outbreaks of it in badgers. And where badgers are free of major outbreaks of the disease, so are cattle, and vice versa. It is true that small outbreaks of the disease occur in cattle in parts of the country where the disease has not been demonstrated in badgers. And it is also true that the *means* by which badgers pass the disease to cattle (if they do) has not been shown. It might be that in the field cattle give the disease to badgers, but not vice versa, or that both badgers and cattle are infected by the disease from a source mutual to each species, but that badgers do not give it to cows.

In the absence of evidence to support these possibilities, the only course of action has quite reasonably seemed to be to kill infected cows and all badgers coming from the immediate vicinity of infected cows, where at least some badgers in that vicinity can be shown to be infected. This gives rise to a very unfortunate part of the badger's relation to the disease: no one can yet reliably tell whether a badger is infected with infectious tuberculosis until it is dead.

The Ministry of Agriculture sees no alternative, therefore, to exterminating badgers if they live close to infected cattle and if (and only if) badgers have been shown to be infected in the immediate area. Thus some 'innocent', uninfected badgers may well be killed in the process. However, there is some evidence that a badger sett which has been cleared of badgers can later be re-established with badgers which do not then themselves become infected.

Much research is now going on into the possible connections between tuberculosis in badgers and cattle. And there is some possibility that a means may be found of vaccinating badgers against the disease.

As usual, the vegetarian is free to say that if we gave up milk, cheese and meat (which are all products of dairy farms) in our diet, the badger with tuberculosis could not conceivably be in conflict with human requirements. However, present policies may well ultimately eliminate the disease in badgers, which could easily be argued as making the policies beneficial to badgers, though delivering such a vaccine might be seen by some as a threat to their very wildness.

The competition between ourselves and seals is even less solidly understood, let alone proved, than that between ourselves and badgers. The grey seal has doubled its population in Scottish waters in the past few years. It eats fish which we also want to harvest and it carries a disease which reduces the commercial value of cod. But we have massively overfished some of the same waters which the seal uses, and the seal takes many fish which we do not want. In other words, the overfishing by people ought not to be confused with the predation by seals, even if our greed in the past now puts us in conflict with seals. It also looks as though the incidence of codworm has not increased in proportion to the rise in seal populations, and may not diminish proportionately with controlled seal numbers; codworm may not have much to do with seal numbers at all.

Research is going on into seal ecology, and may well clear up the relationship between seals and the populations and health of fish which we also want to exploit. In the meantime, though there is not much solid evidence in favour of the annual, now limited, seal cull, we are free to speculate whether the outcry which it causes is really justified. As harvesting of animal produce goes, the seal cull is pretty civilized. So much publicity and attention has been devoted to the deaths of a few thousand seal pups that they are dispatched with a good deal of care. But many devoted seal 'lovers' are fuelled not merely by indignation but also by milk, cheese, yoghurt and meat which have, arguably, a very much greater quotient of misery attendant upon their production than does seal fur.

In conclusion, we can say that we hunt, befriend, admire, dread, eulogize or torture animals with scant regard for their real needs or natures. While one person acquires information painstakingly in the field, using the best available technology and brain-power, another wilfully ignores the valuable insights being gained. However, the awesome pressures which we profligately impose on this planet become more and more obvious and threatening to wildlife. There is a corresponding groundswell of feeling in favour of not further imposing on animals our sporting whims since animals are now perceived to have a spiritual and aesthetic value to us which is ill reflected by killing as many of them as possible.

We are beginning to realize that wildlife is not now so abundant that we should plunder it for fun; rather, its very scarcity and the fragility of its position in the modern world demand that we search our consciences very hard when we interfere in the lives of the animals with whom we share the country. We have learned a great deal about animals in the past twenty years, and will be learning much more in the future. Almost all of it supports the view that we should leave animals alone whenever possible. They seldom threaten us, and are a richer resource to us when we let them live their lives without our interference.

6

CAMPAIGNERS

In the summer of 1982, 5,000 people turned out for a demonstration against the animal experimentation going on at the government's chemical warfare research centre at Porton Down. Several got inside the grounds, led by the new wave of anti-vivisectionists who run the British Union for the Abolition of Vivisection (BUAV). These are the 'hard' campaigners who have cut a swathe through the three or four bodies which have command of the funds and the loyalties of the nineteenth-century animal campaign bodies. They have not been noticeably patient in their politicking within the bodies which they want to control; but then they were taking over from people who had indulged in plenty of careful discussion, and were now in the mood for action.

There is now a large 'left' flank which gingers up the establishment of animal welfare bodies. It ranges from the rough grouping known as the Animal Liberation Front (ALF), which has no formal existence, through groups like Animal Aid to the newly radical BUAV, or the slightly more sedate National Anti-Vivisection Society. No one is supposed to know too much about ALF; its activities are avowedly illegal, and the visible tip of its iceberg, the veteran animal welfare campaigner Ronnie Lee, is on view only because he has eschewed illegal activities for the time being in order to be the Front's spokesman.

The ALF is not interested in argument or in politics, except in the sense that publicity – at which its members have proved themselves adept – constitutes both. It is composed of people who want action, or of people who may spend some of their time on more conventional activities but occasionally like to put on the cape of the masked raider and take matters into their own hands. This usually consists of breaking into and stealing animals from laboratories or factory farms.

In April 1982, following a pattern established ever since its foundation in 1976 from other unnamed groups, over a hundred ALF people broke into Life Research Laboratories Ltd at Stock in Essex. It was a classic ALF operation against a commercial research laboratory which works on the development and testing of commercial products. The press turned out in force, obeying the summons to the rendezvous which had been arranged in swift, furtive meetings with a man called 'John' either in pubs or in their own offices. The next day a wide gamut of papers carried the story of the raid, with pictures of masked men cradling their haul – five beagle dogs, three of which were later recovered by police – in their arms. After car chases, around sixty people were kept at Chelmsford police station until the evening, and the majority were kept overnight. The police found that their captives were an awkward bunch: they refused to eat meat or eggs. It seems that the police, in common with many people who would never do such things themselves and would normally disapprove of anything like burglary or robbery, are oddly sympathetic towards the ALF.

Angela Walder of the BUAV, with whom the police have had many dealings, was on hand at her office in Charing Cross Road to help pressmen and police with information, being known to both parties to have an understanding with the ALF people, and being trusted by the press and the police alike to know what she is talking about. Angela is a ferocious defender of animals, but a subtle operator as well. Every Sunday sees her and a dedicated band of supporters maintaining a constant barrage of megaphoned criticism against the traders in Club Row, near Brick Lane, where for a century or more pet animals have been sold from stalls. She and her associates are now under orders to stay on their own side of the road, while the traders carry on their trade on theirs. (The Club Row battle has been won since this was written.) Every now and again she has been hauled in by the police, and on one occasion – when she claims that she was not resisting arrest – her arm was so severely wrenched that even now, two years later, it is in a form of splint. She is taking the policeman concerned to court for the injury.

But her transactions with the police are curious: she will not compromise with them at all, and yet they seem to be content to deal with her. She has sent all the policemen of some of the East End stations copies of animal welfare literature, so that they know why she is doing what she is. In early June 1982 she and some friends occupied the psychology department at Oxford University in protest against animal experimentation (a century before them, Ruskin had resigned from the University on the issue of vivisection). They agreed to leave only when the police who had been sent in to get them had read some animal welfare literature (and even so, they merely decamped to the zoology department).

She is an extremist. She wears badges of dogs in her lapel; she insists that total abolition of animal experimentation is what she is fighting for; she seems to give up every waking minute to the cause of animal welfare, and seems never happier than when she is giving people who give animals a hard time, or those who defend such people, an even harder time, and often in very direct confrontation. But it is Angela Walder who contributed a guest editorial to the journal *Pain*, at the invitation of Professor Patrick Wall, in which, in very cool and measured terms, she implored scientists to consider very carefully the value of what they are doing and the way that they use animals in their work. She is a valued member of the Committee for the Reform of Animal Experimentation, and is also one of the few sources of pooled information on the animal research laboratories and the work that goes on inside them.

In all this she is uniquely equipped, as a one-time laboratory animal technician – a very particular kind of kennel maid, with many different species in her charge – who has herself held a licence under the 1876 Act because there were times when it was her job to deliver the *coup de grâce* to animals when the researchers themselves were off duty. She knows the standard practices of laboratories and, very importantly, she also knows the kind of abuses, mistakes and disasters which are bound to occur in any organization, and which in the case of animal research laboratories are usually and conveniently shrouded in mystery.

She is under no illusions about the power of the science and industry lobbies which are ranged against her campaign, or about the police and their capacity for bending or ignoring the law when it suits them. But for as long as the movement needs nerve and leadership she will provide it, while also being a surprisingly respected voice in the political background as well.

The ALF activist can expect gaol sooner or later for his or her cause. Ronnie Lee, for instance, is now the official spokesman of the organization and arranges many of its press contacts, which are close if complicated. He has served gaol sentences twice: in 1975 for damaging a laboratory and a seal-hunting boat, and in 1977 for stealing mice from a laboratory. However, he says that he does not endorse some of the more extreme activities of people claiming to be ALF supporters, and that one or two violent individuals have had to be drummed out of the group.

'But this is not an organization,' he insists. 'It is a state of mind.' He says that there are around fifty cells of ALF supporters around the country, almost all of them cooking up schemes – usually raids on laboratories or factory farms. The idea seems to be to make such operations as expensive as possible to their owners by causing damage and by making extravagant security methods necessary. But sometimes the targets are not buildings or commercial property, and then the behaviour of the ALF is far more suspect and bewildering to people who might otherwise support them.

In 1980 and 1981 there were reports of ALF attacks on the personal property of scientists who had used animals in their research, or who the ALF believed had done so. Even in those cases where their targets had been, in the ALF's terms, well chosen, there was considerable anxiety about whether it was legitimate to spray their cars and houses with slogans. Worse, there were also reports that some ALF people had been telephoning scientists at home and threatening them and their families. This was clearly a crazy tactic which could not have been better calculated to alienate potential support as well as bringing into question whether – there being several other methods of making the point and alleviating animal misery – the ALF was not deliberately pitting itself against society.

It has been a common jibe that people who campaign for animals are emotionally peculiar. Certainly, I have never met a bright animal rights campaigner who did not admit that among the first requirements is to be eccentric and dedicated. But that is true of anyone who has the wit to see that things are not as they ought to be, and the ability to stand aside from the mainstream of society and to heap obloquy on the majority, the wrong-doers. The sensible, the wholly sane and ordinary, the well-adjusted, the middle-of-the-road person (where that rare being exists) may make a good and brave campaigner for right and good if sufficiently motivated and if enough other people are swimming in the same tide. But to discern the evils in society and to fight against them usually require a kind of distance from it. We have great need of this sort of 'dottiness'. And it can certainly be found among the current crop of the movement's leaders.

Sue Merrikin, for instance, has been running a hostel in Nottingham, where a variety of people who find difficulty getting a home on their own can share a house together. Her house is also the centre of a great network of people who are trying to eliminate pet-stealing from Nottingham and the Midlands, where it has become epidemic, and where there is a strong suspicion that many of the cats and dogs will end up in laboratories (which are under no legal obligation to check or record the source of their animals). She has been a part-time van driver for the RSPCA and retains a good deal of affection for the society. But around 1979 she found that she was getting too impatient with the normal channels of reform in animal abuse: she wanted to strike out in a more radical and direct way.

These new activities landed her in the Crown Court in Doncaster in February 1982 on a charge of robbery. The events leading up to the case were a perfect example of the kinds of difficulties which face both the new and the old wave of animal welfarists, and especially when they find themselves almost in competition.

The RSPCA inspector for the Doncaster region, Terry Spamer, is the ideal person for the job. He has the instincts of a policeman: his suspicions are easily aroused where animals are concerned, but he likes to be sure of his ground before he acts. When he does act, it is with a good deal of deliberation and determination. He had not been in the post long before he realized that, like his predecessor, he would be having a good deal to do with a man called Ellis Rafe Fox, who had for years been running some sort of animal-trading business from his mother's house. The Foxes are apparently a well-known animal-dealing family, and various members have had pet shops and market stalls in the region over the years. But for a while it was clear that Ellis Fox was no longer operating from his mother's house, and no one quite knew where he was. It turned out that he had bought a farm at Askern (it was rumoured that he paid cash). The news came because a man had turned up at the farm to buy a budgerigar for his child's birthday, and had been so disturbed by what he saw that he got in touch with the RSPCA.

Terry Spamer made the first of many visits to Ellis Fox, and began amassing evidence of a very extraordinary sort of animal-keeping (it could not be called farming). Ellis Fox kept goats, pigs, dogs, cats, ferrets (by the barrel-load) and sheep in conditions of incredible squalor. Finally, early in 1981, Terry Spamer, the local police and health officials raided Highfield Farm. According to the *Sheffield Morning Telegraph*, they found Ellis Fox in a barn with

three West Indians and three Asians.

On the floor was a goat's fleece, a bag of intestines, a bag of blood, a goat's and sheep's heads. Fox admitted killing a sheep and goat by slitting their throats with a knife.

In the subsequent trial at Doncaster Magistrates Court in May 1981, the prosecution said, according to the *Telegraph*, that 'Fox admitted he had a good trade selling live sheep and goats to Mohammedans.' To give an impression of what the place was like, the paper reported that the police found

18 pigs, some lame, standing up to their bellies in excreta; bins of decomposing offal with maggots, which Fox said was to feed his ferrets; sheep's heads, skulls and bones with poultry pecking at them; a cage full of flea-ridden cats with some dead ones amongst them.

The total tally was

300 poultry, 200 budgies, 40 guinea pigs, 40 rabbits, 100 ferrets, 42 cats, 10 dogs, 50 goats, 18 pigs and 2 bullocks ... Asked about the cats and dogs, Fox replied: 'I got them from my contacts. They were going to be for experimentation, but they are not healthy enough.'

On his fifty-three admitted charges of cruelty, contraventions of slaughterhouse regulations and having a pet shop without a licence, Ellis Fox was fined a total of £1,500, disqualified from keeping dogs for ten years and banned from holding a pet-shop licence.

While Ellis Fox was before the magistrates, Sue Merrikin and several others went to the farm in a hired van, and – having told Fox's girlfriend (there with her young baby) to stay in a room – took various animals from the farm. One of them was an Alsatian whose chain had been so tight that it had eaten its way into the animal's neck, and had done so over such a long period that the skin had grown over the chain.

It did not take the police long to find Sue Merrikin and charge her. The police inspector involved, knowing that he had an eccentric on his hands, took her home to his family and was thus able to make sure that she would be able to eat her 'health food' as he called it – namely, a meat-free diet. Eventually they charged her with robbery. The case was set for November 1981.

However, in the meantime Terry Spamer and the police had been busy at Highfield Farm again. In July and August 1981, they raided Mr Fox and assembled another batch of charges. This time, they hoped, they would begin to get somewhere. The law allows that a person who has once been convicted of cruelty to animals can be banned from animal-keeping altogether. They believed that this time the catalogue of abuse was so large that this must be the outcome. And so in November 1981 they presented evidence at Doncaster Magistrates Court. They said that raids had revealed goats and sheep with broken legs; a sheep with a prolapsed uterus; another with apparent prolapse of the anus; a goat with a chronic skin disease which made it look as though it had an elephant's hide; a goat in a terminal condition in a gulley (it had to be put down); a dead goat which was shown later to have lungworm; a goat which was entangled in barbed wire and had to be released.

The majority of the charges were for offences involving goat-keeping, and, incredible though it must seem, the defence spokesman – said by local lawyers and newspapermen to be an expensive barrister – managed to claim that not only was Ellis Fox a poor man who had financial difficulties, but was also a person who had simply been overcome by the goat-keeping side of his business and had let the whole enterprise slip on that account. The magistrates swallowed this tale, and sentenced Ellis Fox to a fine of £500 in total, with £100 costs, and disqualified him from goat-keeping for ten years. Dogs and goats were now to be safe from Ellis Fox for a while.

Terry Spamer was clearly disappointed with the outcome. He left the court still determined that the strange enterprises of Ellis Fox ought to be curbed, for by then he had become personally involved. He certainly had come to believe that there was something in the gossip that there was a pet-stealing ring of some sort on his patch and that somehow he was upsetting them. His van had its tyres slashed and bricks were thrown through the window of his house.

'An RSPCA inspector sees more cruelty every day, day in and day out, than most people see in a lifetime,' he says. But he does not believe that Ellis Fox or many of his other quarry are sadistic; rather, that they are more hopeless or stupid. 'I think Fox trades in animals the way you or I might trade in second-hand cars, and that's how he treats them,' he states. He has had cases of people trying to kill unwanted dogs by driving nails into their eyes in the hope of penetrating the brain, of people attacking dogs with hammers and, in one case, a man who chopped up a dog with an electric saw and sold chunks of the corpse as pet food round the local pubs. Terry Spamer must do his best to investigate the torrent of complaints he receives, which he does by using the force of his uniform as best he may, and by judicious use of the Ways and Means Act, a good understanding of which is essential to an RSPCA inspector, especially since the RSPCA have no more formal powers than any other citizen.

At the same time, the ALF are impatient with Terry and people like him. 'They are always saying that I don't do enough,' he says. 'But I have to have evidence, which they don't bother with. They can make wild allegations if they like. I can't.'

The ALF and Terry Spamer certainly have a different point of view about the raid the ALF made on Highfield Farm on the day of Ellis Fox's first trial. He thinks that though they liberated some dogs, they were also depriving him of evidence which he could have used to get Ellis Fox back in court very quickly indeed. The ALF merely felt that Ellis Fox would have been bound to get rid of the animals very soon after the case (especially as he was likely to be disqualified from keeping dogs, as indeed he was), and that it was therefore essential that they be rescued before anyone else, perhaps of Fox's sort, was able to relieve him of some of his stock.

A week after Ellis Fox's second case, Sue Merrikin was in the Crown Court in the same building, accused of robbing Ellis Fox and his girlfriend of various dogs. She put on her best clothes, made herself up prettily and was generally very conscious that she must at all costs appear calm and ordinary, though she is well aware that she is on a short fuse where animal abuse is concerned and is quite happy that this is the case. The northern stringers from the *Sun* and other national papers sat alongside the local pressmen and settled in for a trial which was bound to last at least a couple of days.

Sue Merrikin admitted taking the dogs but denied that it was robbery. Sue had always said that there was no violence used against Ellis Fox's girlfriend and young baby, and she insists that she would never have countenanced any sort of viciousness against them. Indeed, it has sometimes troubled her how nervous, and therefore potentially unreliable, some of the ALF people have appeared to be on raids. She has felt that it might be possible one day that she would have to intervene to call off an action if it showed any signs of getting out of hand.

However, the argument about what actually happened that day never got far. The prosecution put its case within a couple of hours, and the judge ordered an adjournment. When he came back, it was to say that Sue's conduct at Highfield Farm that day did not add up to robbery. Though reprehensible, it had not had, he said, the required element of violence or threat, or of dishonest purpose. He said that a charge of robbery was not appropriate. He then asked Sue Merrikin to come into the witness box (and nearer to him than she had been in the dock) and delivered the kind of talking-to that makes a court of law, at least sometimes, a heartening place to visit. He said that English law insisted that everyone had rights. The girl at Highfield Farm had the right to expect that people would not be going around 'mob-handed'. But, he said, so did Sue Merrikin have rights, and in particular the right not to be charged wrongly. He said also that in having been treated properly and decently, Sue herself was put under a very clear obligation to respect other people's rights, just as hers had been respected. He bound her over to keep the peace for twelve months and threw the prosecution out.

So Sue Merrikin was free after all, and went back to the work which seems to her most important: running the network of people who are doing their best to collate evidence of pet-stealing rings in the Midlands. It is a campaign which has been gaining respectability recently, and is now supported by people who would be rather shocked at the ALF connections of some of their collaborators.

It is certain that pet-stealing is a serious problem. Spamer in the early days of the investigation was told by Fox that some of his animals were for sale to laboratories, which explained the presence of dozens of fully grown cats on his 'farm'. (There were also, at one point, dozens of kittens, many of them with dreadful signs of diseases, including some sort of green mucous covering over their eyes.) But it is notoriously difficult to track down the sources of animals that find their way into laboratories. However, in recent years two bizarre incidents have received publicity which reinforces the activities of Sue Merrikin and others and goes a long way towards making her case respectable.

The first took place in 1978 when a mostly teenage gang of small-time burglars was convicted of stealing pets of all sorts around various South Yorkshire mining communities; they included goats (presumably for the Muslim meat trade) and other animals for the research market. Police inquiries led them to a Leeds University laboratory, where a dog called Nippy, which had been snatched from its home street (it had been a stray which adopted a family), was discovered.

The second incident took place in October 1980, when an ALF raid on a laboratory liberated a dog, whose photograph was then published in the papers. Delighted to hear news that the dog, which they recognized, had been discovered, its previous owners were put in touch with its ALF liberators. A rendezvous was made at a motorway service area, and the previous owners and the dog were reunited. (It was clear to everyone who was there, including a journalist from the newspaper which had first published the picture, that because of the dog's recognition they were indeed its owners.)

Naturally enough, Terry Spamer of the RSPCA knows a good deal about the pet-stealing scene on his patch. He is also better informed about what people such as Sue Merrikin know than his bosses at the Society's headquarters might like to be aware of, mostly through convenient anonymous phone calls from ALF people, but he is scrupulous about the respectability that being an RSPCA man confers. When he rings the police for support, they give it; often it must be the same policemen who will later be chasing ALF people.

However, it is the case that there is much better support for the ALF at all levels of society than anyone might dare to admit publicly. Ronnie Lee has often been told that an animal liberator does not belong in gaol.

The newspapers clearly enjoy the ALF activities. The *Daily Telegraph* always carries long reports of ALF activities, and splashed February's raid on Life Research on its front page with two pictures. The popular papers are always keen to describe in lurid terms arguments put by both sides. In the *Daily Telegraph*, the laboratory's spokesman said that 'these people were not animal lovers. They were thugs in Nazified uniforms [balaclavas to cover their faces] and the law of the land should deal with them.' But he had less than an inch of column in which to put his case, while the ALF emerged, if only tacitly, as some sort of peculiar heroes. And it seems as if there is a degree of support for the ALF from people who would be horrified at direct action of a similar sort if undertaken, say, by trade unionists in prosecution of a wage claim, or by a terrorist group seeking some political change.

There is a feeling, not altogether rational but understandable, that suggests that when people are in dispute with one another it really ought to be possible for them to keep their argument at the level of parley, and that we must therefore support the strong social taboos against resorts to violence. With animals the difference is largely that the debate was never equal: the liberators are doing what only people can do, and they are doing it on behalf of animals; the ALF is doing nothing to its own obvious advantage in liberating creatures. Moreover, so long as there is no damage to people, the papers feel fairly safe in not condemning the raiders too strongly. Whenever the ALF is reported to be damaging the homes of scientists or threatening them or their families, the papers take a very different line.

The radical activists have not restricted their activities to working in the field. They have links with almost all the animal welfare bodies, and many of them are said to have been packing the old-established societies and either influencing them for change or actually succeeding in taking them over. Animal welfare campaigners can now join groups like Animal Activists, Animal Aid or the very determined Hunt Saboteurs Association (HSA), which has close links with ALF, and others which appear to have members in older societies like the BUAV, the National Antivivisection Society (which is rather milder than the BUAV), the League Against Cruel Sports and the RSPCA. The *Shooting Times* of 6 September 1979 caught the mood of the problem in its own field:

UNHOLY ALLIANCE WITH ANARCHISTS

In case any field sportsmen and women are sitting back, breathing relaxed sighs of relief that the advent of a Conservative government has apparently removed the immediate threat to sports, they would do well to realize that our common enemy is working full time and with increasing vigour as they find themselves thwarted and frustrated.

One, possibly the most alarming, development is the apparent alliance between the so-called Animal Liberation Front, the Hunt Saboteurs and the anarchist movement.

A document calling itself the *Anarchist Fortnightly, Freedom* ... contains a review on animal liberation ... ALF clearly states that it will continue to 'destroy property used to oppress non-human animals ...'

While we accept that individuals are perfectly entitled to oppose field sports by any legitimate means available to them, and while we accept that HSA is violent and disruptive, we doubt if even their members care to be so closely associated with the Animal Liberation Front who, in their extreme frenzy, are prepared to be linked with anarchists.

We suggest that even the 'respectable' field sports opposition groups appear to be lying with some extremely dubious bed-partners.

Whatever problems the hunt saboteurs might now cause in their tricky alliance with anarchists, the fuss was nothing compared with what the takeover of the BUAV by radicals sparked off. The BUAV radicals were opposed to any policy on animal experimentation which looked even remotely as though gradual reform was tolerable. Thus there could be no support of any kind, however temporary, hedged about or codicilled, for the Halsbury Bill as amended by the House of Lords Select Committee. Events came to a head during 1980 when the presidency fell vacant. The radicals had their own ideas as to who should be the new president.

They indulged in a classic piece of entryism, exploiting the society's constitution, which ordained that only members present at the Annual or Extraordinary General Meetings could vote on such a major issue. There were last-minute manoeuvrings by the reformist, or gradualist, elements on the committee and staff to have the rules changed. At one point they seriously attempted to have the society reborn in a new form, intact but for the change in the voting procedure, but were thwarted by legal difficulties. In attempting these ruses, they were acting perfectly decently by their lights, preserving the funds and respectability (such as it was) painfully accumulated over the years by a body whose complexion its benefactors knew. Why, the reformists asked, should the radicals inherit the advantages of an organization which they had done nothing to build historically and with whose historic methods they did not sympathize (even if the eventual aims were shared)? For their part, the radicals merely insisted that the BUAV had scored precious few triumphs in its long years (bar perhaps the achievement, and the NAVS had done this as well, of a fund for the research of alternatives). The radicals' view was that the day of the 'wets' was done. As one of the radicals, Mrs Jean Pink, the founder of Animal Aid, said, the organization had an income of £33,000 a year, and she was bound to be keen to see a radical executive and committee in command of BUAV's annual £300,000.

Ask pertinent questions as they might, the reformers were ousted. There were attempts to draft Richard Ryder as a potential presidential candidate, but they failed. In the end a radical was installed. The lost legal battle against the radical insurgents had cost £10,000 in 1980 alone. Along the way their determination to sweep away the old guard led the radicals into some grotesque insensitivity of behaviour: the first action of the new committee in January 1981 was to sack the former general secretary, David Paterson (who ran and still runs the Humane Education Trust, dedicated to inculcating more ecologically aware educational methods, especially in science). They did so amid a welter of false accusations, and subsequently had to concede to an industrial inquiry that their dismissal of him had been precipitate and unfair. The BUAV had to pay £1,200 compensation, which would have been much greater if David Paterson had not, upon losing his job, immediately found other ways of earning a living. The radicals probably thought the money well spent: they emerge as thoroughly tough characters in this encounter.

Membership under the new brigade rocketed upwards from 2,000 to 10,000 in eighteen months, and it was clear that the new BUAV had caught the imagination of many young people.

They began an aggressive and loud advertising campaign with posters both paid for and fly-posted, stepped up the campaign against the Club Row pet traders, and took on Angela Walder as scientific adviser.

Throughout this period the RSPCA, the doyen animal welfare body, had its own troubles, closely mirroring those of the BUAV. The society, not then royal, was founded during the pre-Victorian flowering of moral feeling about animals. It was a minority cause, but it had its powerful exponents, and even *The Times*, initially a doughty opponent of this new assault on a man's freedom to do as he will, came round. The society was born on 16 June 1824. An odd assortment of Anglican vicars, Quakers and others met at Old Slaughter's Coffee House in St Martin's Lane, having been convened by the Reverend Arthur Broome, from east London. Among them was the garrulous, brave, duelling Irish landowning MP, Richard 'Hairtrigger Dick' Martin.

Though the society was soon to receive the royal blessing of Princess Victoria, and has since attracted a certain amount of respectable as well as of decent feeling, there has always been occasional and sometimes loud dissension within its ranks. However, each side in the RSPCA dispute misunderstands the other. Each is obsessed with the other's crude political alignments (which are indeed often quite clear), when what really alienates the two sects is a powerful mesh of difference which ranges from generation (often the *old* guard is just that, as are the *young* radicals) to background (the reactionaries by and large are rural or suburban, the radicals urban). Many of the reactionaries are not establishmentarian because they are rich, however: many of them are clinging to 'respectability' with great tenacity precisely because they are neither successful nor young (and this sort of person has always been ferociously conservative). Nor are many of the radicals ferociously left-wing: many have educated themselves into a concern for animals by a route which does not at all make them socialist. Indeed, the political left wing has shown little interest in such issues: a *Time Out* appreciation of the animal liberation movement quoted Paul Foot, a member of the Socialist Workers'

Party, as saying, 'I am not in favour of inhumanity to animals and [am] instinctively against factory farming, but I am in favour of the slaughter of animals for meat. To say mankind can survive on a handful of brown rice and bananas is reactionary.' This would of course infuriate the real reactionaries of the RSPCA, who would more likely stress that to suggest such a diet was dangerously close to world revolution by dottiness.

The divisions within the twenty-three members of the governing council of the RSPCA have never been particularly simple and have got a good deal more complicated recently. For several years there has been intense rivalry for control of this body, with the society's £7 million budget at its behest, and the rivalry is well represented by two of the major figures within the organization. The Conservative MP Miss Janet Fookes is a former chairman of the council, and is widely regarded as the archetypal reactionary face of the RSPCA. But Miss Fookes, who campaigns for prison reform as well as for animal rights, has often been a bravely outspoken House of Commons opponent to hunting, and has thus shared a radical line on what has sometimes been the dominating issue within the RSPCA (though she would not of course condone the kind of disruption that the radicals espouse privately). And the other face of the RSPCA, its radical wing, is spearheaded by Richard Ryder, a thoughtful, persistently cool campaigner who is a clinical psychologist at an Oxford hospital, something of a bibliophile, and widely believed to have Liberal political ambitions.

The real difficulty of the old guard was to see the youngsters who were besieging their society, which the young characterized as a 'rest home for retired majors', as nothing but troublesome left-wingers. They did not notice either that the extremists in the RSPCA were not ordinary political people or that the youngsters also had a rather powerful case.

The society had dramatically failed to keep pace with the sorts of concerns which worried many young people in the field of animal welfare. There were fox-hunting RSPCA members; there were owners of factory farms; there were people who might be vociferous about urchins abusing cats in the street but were themselves wholly indifferent to the sufferings in research laboratories and happily wear the make-up tested on the animals there. None of these people can seriously claim to have thought through their commitment to animal welfare; but then many of them were and are kindly, not particularly philosophical people for whom the current mores of the mass society (especially as represented by the established and acknowledged arbiters of decent behaviour) matter far more than some new-fangled notions of animal rights as espoused by unruly extremists who were prepared simultaneously to change an ancient pattern of sport and recreation in the hunting field, undermine the basis of food production in the nation (factory farming), deny women their traditional decoration (make-up tested on animals), and wanted to see an end to such innocent and traditional pleasures as visiting the zoo and the circus.

The rows had reached such a point in the early seventies that in 1973 Charles Sparrow, QC, was asked to conduct a Congress-style inquiry into the ferocious brew that the society had become, and especially to hear out what the Reform Group (as the radicals called themselves) wanted to say. In 1974 he published his account of the inquiry's findings:

> We were quite unprepared for the abandon with which some members assailed the council of the society and, indeed, the society itself. Again and again members made a disclaimer of any desire to create bad feeling within the society, and would launch into a torrent of the most bitter accusation. Charges of dishonesty, lying and utter indifference to the interests of animals were the small change of our open sessions.

The Sparrow report decided that the society's main troubles lay with a divided council. The headquarters staff at Horsham had done as well as possible under the strain of such potent divisions in the governing body, but nothing could be done about the divisions: the radicals continued to make inroads into the society's remarkably small membership (more people identify with the society by filling its collection boxes and making legacies than ever bother to sign a membership form), they constituted a powerful element amongst the 38,000 members.

In 1979 the radicals secured for Richard Ryder the presidency of the Council, and have always since then either been in the majority or represented a power bloc which could not be ignored. They succeeded in making the RSPCA take on board the kind of policies which put it firmly in a respectable modern tradition of animal welfare: it now opposes factory farming, circuses, all but the best zoos, hunting and most animal experimentation, though of course it still refuses to sanction any sort of illegal activity and keeps its voice deliberately moderate.

The old guard were still seething at some of the activities and attitudes of the young radicals (though many of them had accepted that the new policies were the least that should be at the masthead of a serious society dedicated to the prevention of cruelty to animals) when in 1979 the crunch came with the new Conservative government offering two senior members of the RSPCA seats on their new Ministry of Agriculture, Fisheries and Food Farm Animal Welfare Council. The radical council refused to allow the officers to accept, while the Minister of Agriculture insisted that the invitation had not been ex officio. The opposing factions divided along classic lines: the radicals thought that the RSPCA should not parley with what they believed would be a whitewash body; the traditionalists were delighted that the society was being taken seriously enough to be invited to sit at the high table. The old guard had a distaste for the willingness with which the radicals were happy to slight a Tory administration.

At a fraught Extraordinary General Meeting the radicals just failed to make their views prevail. Moreover, it seems that during 1980 the more staid faction of the RSPCA managed quite successfully to regain control of the society. The papers had a ball. Here was British society in full flow: Young Turk and Old Ducks were at war. A Tory MP of the old school, Sir Freddie Burden, a former chairman of the society, was snapped collaring young Richard Ryder at the rostrum. Among the animal lovers, the fur was flying.

But by 1981 there were deeper problems within the society. The *Daily Mail* had been making dramatic disclosures about the lifestyle of Julian Hopkins, the society's executive director. Read carefully, the charges amounted to very little more than slightly untactful expenditure in a charitable organization: the council appeared to have been allowing Mr Hopkins the kind of perks more appropriate to a commercial manager than to the head of a body dealing in widow's mites.

Much worse than this, it seems that relations at the society's headquarters were very poor. The divisions within the society's membership were reflected within the staff and officers. There appears to have been little diplomacy at work on either side. And there seems to have been too little thought given to curbing expenditure: the society was appeasing the radicals by spending large sums of money on campaigns which suited them, while simultaneously spending money on the inspectorate, always the favourites of the traditionalists, as well. Inspectors in the field like Terry Spamer mourned the rifts within the society and fervently wished that the thing would blow over.

By early 1982 it was clear that the society could not afford the split which it had allowed to develop. It was losing £1 million a year and had seen several senior staff members dispatched or lost. The society's treasurer, Mrs Rachel Smith, who had had no sympathy with the radicals and had been most vociferous against them in the 1980 debacle over the Farm Animal Welfare Council, joined forces with the current president, Anelay Hart, to undertake an inquiry into the operation of the society's headquarters. It was widely rumoured that they were surprised and saddened by what they learned.

It seemed at last to the radicals that responsible and senior traditionalists were coming round to the realization that the RSPCA's management was simply not adequate to the strains imposed on it by the honest, but wide and occasionally fierce, differences of opinion with it, and that the society simply had not had the kind of intelligent 'civil service' to handle the sort of politics to which it was bound to be subject during a period in which ideas about animal welfare were changing so speedily. In the end, Julian Hopkins was fired from his job, and the RSPCA attempted to find a way of conducting its business with less crippling losses. Clearly it will have great difficulty reconciling its divisions, and its compromises will always be uneasy. Almost every leading figure in the society is under attack from some quarter of the membership.

Richard Ryder's leadership did succeed in making its policies a fairly satisfying blend of what the radicals would stop rioting about and what the traditionalists could just manage to swallow. It is a compromise in which the animals still suffer more than anyone could seriously suppose acceptable; but on the other hand it is a compromise which will still probably entice ordinary people – uncommitted and kindly – to put their hand in their pocket and to remember the RSPCA in their wills, without feeling that their money is being used as a subscription for violent revolution.

The old guard pretend that the radical moves will be bad for the society's finances, but in this they are probably underestimating both the change of opinion in the country and the way in which their traditional 'market' of supporters is disappearing. It may be that the hotheads are a better bet for the RSPCA's survival, though that will almost certainly leave a problem for the inspectorate.

The RSPCA's inspectors are really the animals' constabulary, but the wilder radicals are not good at supporting the boys in blue, whether they be of the kind that police people or animals. The inspectors are, however, the heroes of the RSPCA's branches, which are mostly traditional and whose power is significant in an organization which is importantly federal. To some extent, the better the RSPCA is as a campaigning and liberal organization, the greater the chance that its inspectorate will go unloved by its new masters.

The inspectorate is at one and the same time seen as the traditional fund-puller and the part of the RSPCA least appropriate to a campaigning body which would like to change public attitudes. But with losses of £1 million a year the time has come for the RSPCA to reconsider in very serious terms what it wants to try to do for the next quarter-century. Its animal-policeman role is expensive to maintain, and in effect merely gives the human-police a natural home for any animal-buck they want to pass. There is a good argument for suggesting that the ordinary authorities ought not to be allowed this encouragement to ignore their obligation to enforce the laws about animals.

However, this argument is anathema to the traditionalists in the RSPCA who, through the branches, have the greatest contact with the inspectorate and firmly believe it to be the source of the RSPCA's good and respected image, and hence of much of its fundings. It is nevertheless clear that the campaigning role of the RSPCA is of a very different sort than its role as policeman: the one courts eccentricity and controversy; the other is quintessentially authoritarian and respectable.

The council has recently been addressing itself to the question of how to heal the divisions within the society while seeking to redefine its various roles in such a way that the uneasy alliance between RSPCA members can be strengthened. It faces increasing problems as its inspectors protest at cuts in their strength which have already been forced through, while any attempt at further trimming the campaigning radicals at headquarters meets with their well-orchestrated howls of complaint.

Meanwhile, only the naïve believe that the animal liberation movement has become the hostage of a few power-crazed left-wingers. The *Daily Telegraph*, in glorious apoplexy, tried to pursue this in a leader on 1 March 1980 at the height of the RSPCA's troubles:

'Progressive' has long served as a euphemism for the extreme left and its camp-followers. It is, therefore, with something approaching unbelief that we see a self-styled progressive group poised to take over the RSPCA, the archetypal home of respectability tempered by eccentricity. But the facts speak for themselves.

On second thoughts, the matter should occasion little surprise. For is this not the essence of what we have come to know as 'entryism'? The older, more respected and richer an organization, the riper it may be for takeover. Entryists join, keeping their views and intentions well hidden, take on all the chores, seek election to posts for which there is little competition, bring in their fellow-conspirators. Then, hey-ho, the bird is in their hand, name, funds and all. Anything can be politicized. Factory farming can be used as a means of attacking the bona fides of all concerned. Hunting, the fur trade and almost any sphere of activity related to animals can be used as a stick with which to beat the free society.

It is hard to look at *The Animals Film*, a hard-hitting documentary made by a left-wing New Yorker, Victor Schonfeld, without seeing the point of some of this view, however far-fetched it was in the case of the RSPCA. *The Animals Film* is clearly a very important piece of work: it brought and will bring to a mass audience a new realization of the miseries inflicted on animals by war-mongering and profit-seeking man.

However, even the film's poster somehow gave a bit of its game away. 'It's not about them, it's about us,' it said: in other words, we can see what happens to animals as important because it reflects so badly on us as people. And though there were some stretches of the film where we saw dim-witted consumers who clearly had never thought about animals at all, the majority of the piece was about the profiteers and the war-mongers themselves. The implicit message was that these people were now exploiting animals as part and parcel of their exploitation of the masses. The view has a certain logic, but it was a clear case of the intrusion of politics into compassion, and evidence that, as the *Daily Telegraph* said, animals can be used 'as a stick with which to beat the free society'.

And the great difficulty with *that* is that, in all sorts of fields of modern life, a revolt of some form against materialism, war-mongering or animal abuse could all happen far quicker if it were not plagued by a political overtone in which ordinary people feel they cannot work with movements which appear to be so peculiarly resentful against what is, after all, a better way of life than most people have enjoyed, or do enjoy, on the face of the earth. *The Animals Film*, in common with much protest, will do no good if it creates the impression that the exponents of these eccentric views are merely misanthropes whose complaint against society reflects far more on their own psychological miseries than any supposed empathy with the creatures whose cause they espouse, and whose interests – and not any political or even cultural capital – should be at the heart of their concern.

This sort of debate was perfectly encapsulated when Lord Halsbury and Lord Houghton made their speeches in the House of Lords on the Laboratory Animals Protection Bill, which Lord Halsbury and the Research Defence Society introduced and a Select Committee, with Lord Halsbury and Lord Houghton sitting on it, had mauled into something like a humane bill, which was, nonetheless, catastrophically weak in most of the strategic places. Lord Houghton had decided, presumably, that the Bill was as good as it was going to be, and perhaps hoped for improvements in it as it went through the full parliamentary process. Lord Halsbury, presumably, thought (and he had good right to) that most of the research now being done on animals could continue with the new Bill almost as well as under the old, and that therefore its welfare improvements could be welcomed on their merits.

And so on 18 December 1980 Lord Halsbury stood up and said that his Bill was again before their lordships and he believed it to be a good Bill. However, he then launched into a peroration on the subject of the animal welfare campaigners:

We live in abnormal times in which the advocates of minority opinion now feel free to emphasize their opinions by civil commotion and violence at a time when the judiciary seem to have lost their faith in punishment as a deterrent . . .

He described some of the protestors as having 'somewhat disturbed personalities' and being in need of sympathy rather than hostility.

In the middle of the range there are somewhat more neurotic types who are embittered about the subject and resemble the man with a grievance – if you remove his grievance, he only acquires another one; if they could not protest about animals, they would be protesting about putting fluoride into drinking water, or something like that.

Then, at the far end of the spectrum, there are people who are getting on to the border of what is psychotic rather than neurotic and suffering from delusions of persecution, not on behalf of themselves, but on behalf of something else – animals, for instance: a kind of paranoia; one might call it vicarious paranoia. We have lived with this for over 100 years and we know how to live with it. But unfortunately this militant fringe in modern times has been infiltrated by back-street bully types who use what is a good cause as an excuse for violence and vandalism, which is their real objective.

He told a story of how some ALF people disrupted a thanks-giving service held by the Wellcome Trust, which uses phar-maceutical profits to endow further medical research work. 'These people are quite lost to any sense of what is fitting,' he commented, and asked that the magistrates and others take their legal obligations more seriously in the punishment of such people.

And then it was Lord Houghton's turn.

I regret to say that the noble Earl has no understanding at all of the mood, the outlook and desire for idealism and action of the young people of Britain today. With great respect to him, he is 'an old square'. It is not a bit of good lecturing the magistrates and criticizing the judiciary and virtually asking them to send these people to remand homes or institutions for reform and better order and discipline. None of that is going to carry influence with young people. They are disen-chanted with the society which has been created for them by their elders. They do not like what they see; they want to change it. They want to be where the action is . . . I appeal to noble Lords to understand this problem more deeply than it has been presented to them this afternoon by the noble Earl, Lord Halsbury. I felt so indignant when he was speaking that had I been in the House of Commons I would have interrupted him. I should have been rude to him. If I had been handy for the Mace, I should have run away with it. I should have shown my indignation in the same sort of way that young people do when they find there is no other course open to them.

Neither of the noble Lords is quite right, probably. There is something very odd and exciting at work in the tribal theatre that goes on in politics and protest, and it is not much use – except as shorthand – to see it as idealism versus interest; left versus right; young versus old; cosy status quo versus neurotic dissidence. In truth, campaigns and campaigners are a feroci-ous cocktail of all of these. They are what being a human animal is all about: we are the arguing animal above all else.

We are also the political animal. In the 1979 general elec-tion, under the leadership of Lord Houghton as chairman and Clive Hollands (of the Scottish Society for the Prevention of Vivisection) as secretary, the General Election Coordinating Committee for Animal Protection brought together many campaigning bodies to 'put animals into politics' (their slogan). They were successful. Lorries with slogans were parked outside seaside party conferences, candidates canvassed and pressure applied on the manifesto-writers. Certainly, all the parties found that they needed to say something about animal welfare, and any likely government in future will find that it has been committed in advance to do something in the field.

At a local level, the Labour and Liberal parties vie with one another in attempts to forbid fox-hunting on council-owned land, though any Conservative-dominated council always seems to defeat such moves easily. However, there are more and more councils which will not allow animal acts in circuses on their land.

By late 1982, a new, rather more radical committee had been formed to fight the election which, it was speculated, would be called in early 1983. It was uncertain whether the more respectable welfare bodies would like its new tone: the RSPCA could not make up its mind whether to support the venture. What is certain is that between the activists and the parliamentarians and the vast body of public concern for animals, expressed and fuelled by at least four television programmes in the late autumn of 1982, there was a new impetus behind the campaigns to reform the nation's treatment of animals.

The campaigners of the last hundred years may have been richly eccentric, and some of them ferociously egomaniacal. They may have fought with terrible fury among themselves. But they have also put animals on the national agenda.

CONCLUSION

Animals are one of the great mysteries in the world, and we are looking at them in a new light, with a new seriousness. There are plenty of other mysteries in the world, of which we are becoming increasingly wary. We are rediscovering the daunting subtlety of the planet and the rest of Creation among which we must live. We are discovering the alarming damage which we can do. We are beginning to discuss some ideas that seem, to modern Western ears at least, rather curious. They have to do with conducting ourselves with a certain modesty and restraint, especially in respect of those creatures and things which we had previously regarded as there for the taking and using.

E. F. Schumacher used as his subtitle to *Small is Beautiful* the phrase 'economics as if people mattered'. The ecological movement is, broadly speaking, about living our lives as though the rest of Creation mattered. We can take this new tack either because we are aware that by doing so we may survive rather longer ourselves, or because it simply seems the right and proper thing to do. We may even take it because, leaving aside difficult notions of absolute morality, we simply perceive ourselves as being creatures who are rather happier to live by a yardstick other than our own greed and selfishness. This is the impulse which we might take to be very roughly a modern and materialist replacement for (or extension of) some of the qualities which people have found – and still do find – in religion.

This growing awareness of the rest of Creation makes very profound difficulties for ordinarily aware but ordinarily profligate people. Animals are very particularly true examples of what the rest of non-human Creation is like in at least one very important way: they are, superficially, totally in our power. There is not one species of animal (except perhaps those which work in such immense numbers that they can become pestilential, like rats or locusts) over which we do not exert nearly complete control. We can wound, kill and torture them at our whim (and one of the oddest examples in this regard must be the laboratory dog who likes his experimenter, in spite of the pain that is done him). Animals may or may not be like people in all sorts of respects, but they cannot tell us about any similarities where they exist, or disabuse us about those similarities which we might wrongly be suspecting we share with them.

Montaigne thought the similarities between human beings and animals peculiarly close, but not capable of proof:

How does he [man] know, by the strength of his understanding, the secret and internal motions of animals? From what comparison betwixt them and us does he conclude the stupidity he attributes to them? When I play with my cat, who knows whether I do not make her more sport than she makes me? We mutually divert one another with our play. If I have my hour to begin or to refuse, she also has hers.

Montaigne insisted that we do indeed communicate with animals. But Descartes, equally famously, insisted that though animals were very marvellous creations of God, they were automata of an order appropriate to being created by God, and thus far more exciting than the automata produced by humans. He did not deny that creatures could communicate, but he denied them reason; he did not deny them sensation, but insisted that it was a 'bodily sensation' (we, of course, do not understand what such a view can mean: feeling is feeling, in our view). Perhaps he was just concerned to go on with his vivisections and contorted his logic to fit his needs: certainly this is the kind of view attributed to him by modern anti-vivisectors. The Animal Liberation Front vandalized his portrait in an august scientific institution on these grounds.

St Thomas Aquinas, much reviled by animal rights campaigners, said that animals had no moral claim on humans *per se*: God had given us dominion over animals, and he had given free will to us, and not to animals. Thus we are in an altogether different category from animals. However, this view enjoins a responsibility on us in respect of animals: we are required to be charitable.

For my part, I see Descartes's problem: he could see strong distinctions between us and animals, as we all can, and found himself asserting that the difference was that we could both reason and feel in some qualitatively different way. He could only explain what he knew of human beings by supposing something divine in them, a divinity which he was unwilling to allow to animals. Today we would more likely insist that we only reason in a different way, though indeed we continue to abuse animals as if we believed, like Descartes, that their feeling is a matter of indifference.

Bentham, the great Utilitarian, held that it was not at all the differences in reason or the capacity to use language that made animals a charge on humans, but their capacity to suffer. Any evidence that animals can suffer at our hands is evidence towards their being a moral charge on us. Any feeling that they feel because of us equally leads to them being a moral charge on us.

Descartes's position need not worry us. We are not reasoning from his sort of position and premises. Aquinas's is, I believe, worth a lot more attention than people now like to think. Arguing from Bentham and other Utilitarians and rationalists, modern thinkers have developed a system of rights which I consider very dangerous. I do not share Aquinas's view that animals are radically inferior to us, but that is only because I do not share Aquinas's belief that we are not merely (like animals) created by God but also (unlike animals) created in His image. However, I do share with him the view that our obligation to animals is one of charity, just as it is to all creatures. But then I believe moral sense to be a human quality, grown of our brain-power and in particular of our capacity, on the one hand, to empathize with our fellow creatures and, on the other, to discover and then fulfil some larger purpose in life than the prosecution of our interests.

It is the animals' combination of sentiency and inarticulacy which makes them so peculiarly important and enigmatic to us. Their sentiency puts them alarmingly close to us in crucial ways. Their inarticulacy makes them, to their exploiters, rather convenient victims, in that the victim is not constantly impressing on the torturer in its own language that what is going on is deeply unpleasant and similar to what the human would feel if the roles were reversed. At the same time, their inarticulacy is what has motivated their most ardent defenders ('our dumb friends', etc.) and what makes them a very particular charge on us.

It is precisely because animals are otherwise wholly defenceless that we need to help them, even when to do so is to incur the charge that we are thereby taking time out from showing the same care or ferocity of altruism about, say, black South Africans or even the disadvantaged in our society. Moreover, I suspect that there are few of us so busily involved in good works that we cannot find time for a fresh one, and, as has been observed by animal welfare campaigners from very early on, a person who takes the sufferings of animals seriously is doubly likely to be struck by the importance of taking care of their human obligations. Moreover, it is an area in which to do a great deal of good requires only a little inconvenience on our part. This puts a powerful obligation on us to follow the promptings of our consciences.

But if we are to live as though animals mattered, how can we always be sure what this would mean, or how far we ought to take it? Do animals really matter as much as humans? Or is it 'only' as much as retarded humans, as Peter Singer seems to imply when he thought that the only experiment which we ought to contemplate on an animal is the rare one for which we should also contemplate the 'use of a retarded human being' (as though retarded humans did not precisely share with the animals our special care by their inability to claim it for themselves, augmented by an importance which I am quite happy to say attaches to them as being people and not non-human animals). There is room for some hard thinking on this subject, and certainly there has already been some very soft thinking on it. There has been plenty of perfectly respectable expression of gut-feeling, and some of this has been dressed up wrongly as careful thought.

There has, of course, been some good thinking too. But in at least one important way I am out of sympathy with a great deal of it. Several writers, the most well-known example being Peter Singer in his *Animal Liberation*, have discussed the view, which they hold, that animals have rights. I do not agree with this proposition in quite the way that I think they would like one to do. Another writer, Roger Frey, in his *Interests and Rights: The Case Against Animals*, has suggested that animals very definitely do not have rights, and that they have even less claim to them than do people. As I understand it, he makes this case because he believes that animals do not have what he calls interests, by virtue of their lacking some quality of consciousness. Both of these views attempt to intellectualize what is not really a matter for ratiocination, and to attempt to be so rational about such a matter does not ultimately much further it.

Roger Frey's is a supreme example of the silliness of plain philosophy, which prides itself on arguing issues very closely, and often does so as if the ordinary decencies of life were mere algebra. In his case, his close arguing takes him from the view that animals do not have Singer-style rights (which it is quite easy to argue) to the counter-intuitive and absurd position that there does not seem to be a way, on thoughtful grounds, to extend ordinary kindness or compassion to them. He insists that if we watch a film about a slaughterhouse and are put off our meat dinner, then that it is simply a question of squeamishness; and that if the next day we eat our meat dinner, that must be because yesterday's squeamishness does not measure up to today's appetite. But this altogether leaves out the possibility that our squeamishness may enliven our consciences; and while it is the case that one of the weaknesses of conscience is that all too often its power evaporates from one day to the next, that is not at all an argument that matters of the conscience are merely matters either of squeamishness or of rights.

On the one hand, animals do not have rights, in the sense in which these authors use the word. But I know that their suffering is on my conscience when I know that I cause it, and I believe that their suffering ought to be on anybody's conscience.

On the other hand, I do not think that animals have rights, and I do not think that people have them either. At least, they do not have rights in quite the way that many writers suggest.

There is often a quite decent but misguided attempt to make the word rights do too much work and to shift its meaning around in a rather dangerous way. We can use the word rights in two quite different ways. One is that rights are simply there, to be discovered, as though they might be an invisible limb. By this view, we merely have an obligation to do our best to discover, reveal and understand them. By this logic, women, men, slaves, animals, unborn babies, indeed, perhaps anything imaginable, all have or had rights – though they are presumably likely to be different rights in each case – and it behoves intelligent, thoughtful and good people to discover them and then fight for them. Hence, slaves always had the right to be free, but it wasn't until the Wilberforces of the world realized and discovered these rights that they could be fought for.

The other way of using the word, which I prefer, is that people, animals or even things have rights if the relevant authority, preferably with legal support, has bestowed them. Sometimes it can be a very simple thing. In my house, for instance, the cat is accorded the right to come and go as it pleases, which pleasures we take to be evidenced by her waiting at doors and windows signalling – unless we are very wrong – her desires and then, as though to reinforce our belief that her desires were so signalled, doing exactly what one would expect when one opens the door (i.e. going through it).

There is nothing absolute about rights. People ask for them. People bestow them or withhold them. Decent people, struggling to live moral lives, campaign that rights be accorded to all sorts of people and other creatures.

Good people are sensitive about the rights of others and discuss them, and hold themselves to be under an obligation to uphold all sorts of conventions on the subject. Others are very careless about them. Policemen are supposed to be diligent in helping people to live freely within their legal rights. When I am in a benign mood, I try to be good about the cat's rights in this house. But, all too often, people – believing that this, that or the other is possessed of rights – feel secure in committing any outrage or unpleasantness that comes to their mind to secure those rights. They sometimes forget that they ought to persuade others to share their view and to join them in according rights; instead they feel morally free, even obliged, to shove the notion of these rights down our throats. Even if no one else has seen the light, they have discovered such and such a right, as surely as if they had tripped over it in the dark.

This has the peculiar effect of making them claim this or that 'as of right'. Many modern activists, 'fighting' on behalf of poor, disadvantaged, inarticulate humans or on behalf of animals, go so far as to despise charity. They dislike the idea that you and I may choose to be charitable towards the weaker in society, human or animal. They say that charity is always condescending. But it is important to stress that they are wrong. Kindness, charity, acts of voluntary goodness, are among the finest things in the world. Too many right-ists are out to rob us of them.

Richard Ryder, who later became chairman of the RSPCA and has always been a cool campaigner and a subtle propagandist, coined the expression 'speciesism' in the early seventies. It is a useful notion. Drawing on Bentham's idea that animals are worthy of our care because they can suffer, it claims that, whatever inferiorities we can discern in animals compared to humans, they do not constitute a right to treat animals differently from us.

Ryder's essay 'Speciesism: The Ethics of Vivisection' quotes Bentham as he tries to find a way of discussing whether it is reason or articulacy that confers a responsibility on human beings for other creatures:

But a full-grown horse or dog is beyond comparison a more rational, as well as a more conversable animal than an infant of a day, of a week or even a month old. But suppose the case were otherwise, what could it avail? The question is not can they *reason*? Nor, can they *talk*? But can they *suffer*? . . .

Why should the law refuse its protection to any sensitive being? The time will come when humanity will extend its mantle over everything which breathes.

Richard Ryder goes on to argue that the differences between humans and animals never manage to make animals so unlike humans that suffering can be inflicted upon them. 'When,' he asks, 'did a difference justify a moral prejudice?'

So far, in a way, so good. Richard Ryder is free to draw on parallels between the anti-slavery movement and the anti-vivisection or any other animal rights movement, as he does. But should we be happy with this view any more than with Singer-style rights? Leaving aside the jumble of problems associated with whether or not anybody ever does bother to justify prejudices (to do so is to remove their status as prejudices), and even accepting the problems associated with the argument that their capacity to suffer makes creatures a charge on our moral sense, it is easy to argue that animals are less of a charge on people – even good people – than people are.

It is not a strongly logical argument. It simply goes by what ordinary people ordinarily believe and do, and what even good people believe and do. That is to say, very roughly, that they would – pressed to choose – save a human from death or suffering in preference to an animal. This may not be reasonable, but it would be a distinctly odd person who did otherwise. At the same time, however, we do not allow animals any rights in any reasonable sense of the word. Perhaps we should accord them a far more practical respect and, wherever and whenever we can, at least let them live as natural and as unhindered lives as possible.

BIBLIOGRAPHY

Agricultural Research Council, *Jubilee Exhibition Brochure*, 1981.
Annual Review of Agriculture, HMSO, various years.
Attenborough, D., *Zoo Quest to Guiana*, Lutterworth, 1956.
Brambell, F. R. (Chairman), *Report of the Technical Committee to Inquire into the Welfare of Animals Kept under Intensive Livestock Systems*, Cmnd 2896, 1965.
Changing Structure of Agriculture, 1968–75, The, HMSO, 1977.
Dawkins, M., *Animal Suffering*, Chapman and Hall, 1980.
Ehrlich, P. and Ehrlich A., *Extinction: The Causes and Consequences of the Disappearance of Species*, Victor Gollancz, 1982.
Food Standards Committee, *Report on Novel Protein Foods*, HMSO, 1974.
Frey, R. G., *Interests and Rights: The Case against Animals*, Oxford University Press, 1980.
Hall, R., *Animals Are Equal*, Wildwood House, 1980.
Hardin, G., *Biology: Its Principles and Implications*, W. H. Freeman, San Francisco and London, 1961.
Harrison, R., *Animal Machines*, Stuart, 1963.
Home Office, *Statistics of Experiments on Living Animals, Great Britain 1981*, HMSO, 1982.
House of Commons Agriculture Committee, *Animal Welfare in Poultry, Pig and Veal Calf Production, Volume One: Report, Proceedings of the Committee and Appendices; Volume Two: Minutes of Evidence*, HMSO, 1981.
House of Lords, *Report of the Select Committee on the Laboratory Animals Protection Bill (HL)*, HMSO, 1980.
Jordan, B., and Ormrod, S., *The Last Great Wild Beast Show*, Constable, 1978.
Laurance, William W., *Of Acceptable Risk: Science and the Determination of Safety*, William Kaufmann, Los Altos, California, 1976.

Lorenz, K. *On Aggression*, Methuen University Paperbacks, 1967.

McFarland, D. (ed.), *The Oxford Companion to Animal Behaviour*, Oxford University Press, 1981.

Melzack, R., and Wall, P., *The Challenge of Pain*, Penguin Books, Harmondsworth, 1982.

Regan, T. and Singer, P. (eds.), *Animal Rights and Human Obligations*, Prentice-Hall, 1976.

Russell, W. M. S., and Burch, R. L., *The Principles of Humane Experimental Technique*, Methuen, 1959.

Schumacher, E. F., *Small is Beautiful*, Harper & Row, New York, 1975.

Singer, P., *Animal Liberation*, Granada, 1977.

Smith, A., *Animals on View*, Granada, 1979.

Sperlinger, D. (ed.), *Animals in Research: New Perspectives in Animal Experimentation*, John Wiley, New York, 1981.

Teeling-Smith, G., *A Question of Balance: The Benefits and Risks of Pharmaceutical Innovation*, Office of Health Economics, 1980.

Wardle, C., *Changing Food Habits in the UK*, Earth Resources Research, 1977.

Weller, J., *History of the Farmstead*, Faber and Faber, 1982.

USEFUL
ADDRESSES

Animal Liberation Front, Box 190, 8 Elm Avenue, Nottingham.

British Union for the Abolition of Vivisection, 143 Charing Cross Road, London WC2H OEE.

Compassion in World Farming, 20 Lavant Street, Petersfield, Hampshire, GU32 3EW.

Free Range Egg Association (FREGG), 39 Maresfield Gardens, London, NW3 5SG.

Friends of the Earth, 377 City Road, London, EC1V 1NA.

Fund for the Replacement of Animals in Medical Experiments (FRAME), 312A Worple Road, Wimbledon, London, SW20 8QU.

Greenpeace, 36 Graham Street, London, W1 2JX.

National Anti-Vivisection Society Ltd, 51 Harley Street, London, W1N 1DD.

People's Trust for Endangered Species, 19 Quarry Street, Guildford, Surrey.

Royal Society for Nature Conservation, The Green, Nettleham, Lincolnshire LN2 2NR.

Royal Society for the Prevention of Cruelty to Animals, Causeway, Horsham, West Sussex, RH12 1HG.

Royal Society for the Protection of Birds, The Lodge, Sandy, Bedfordshire, SG19 2DL.

Scottish Society for the Prevention of Vivisection, 10 Queensferry Street, Edinburgh, EH2 4PG.

Vegetarian Society, 53 Marloes Road, London, W8 6LA.

Wildfowl Trust, Slimbridge, Gloucestershire, GL2 7BT.

INDEX